TRUTH
OR
DELUSION?

TRUTH
OR
DELUSION?

BUSTING NETWORKING'S BIGGEST MYTHS

IVAN MISNER
MIKE MACEDONIO
MIKE GARRISON

NELSON BUSINESS
A Division of Thomas Nelson Publishers
Since 1798

www.thomasnelson.com

Published in Nashville, Tennessee, by Thomas Nelson, Inc.

Nelson Books titles may be purchased in bulk for educational, business, fund-raising, or sales promotional use. For information, please e-mail SpecialMarkets@ThomasNelson.com.

Givers Gain® is a registered trademark of BNI®

Library of Congress Cataloging-in-Publication Data

Misner, Ivan R., 1956-
    Truth or delusion? : busting networking's biggest myths / Ivan Misner, Mike Macedonio, Mike Garrison.
      p. cm.
    ISBN-13: 978-0-7852-2320-7 (hardcover)
    ISBN-10: 0-7852-2320-7
    1. Business networks. 2. Business referrals. I. Macedonio, Mike.
  II. Garrison, Mike. III. Title.
    HD69.S8M573 2006
    338.8'7—dc22

                                                    2006025854

Printed in the United States of America

06 07 08 09 QWM 5 4 3 2 1

To our children,
Ashley, Cassandra, and Trey;

Robert;

and Alan and Scott,

who've helped us learn the truths and delusions
of fatherhood.

CONTENTS

CONTENTS

CONTENTS

CONTENTS

INTRODUCTION

If you were to ask average businesspersons to list for you the most important ways to build a business, networking would no doubt be on every single list. Yet we don't teach networking in colleges and universities around the world. We give bachelor's degrees in business to students who have no idea how to build their business through networking, because it's not part of the curriculum of most colleges today. Is it any wonder that there are many delusions about networking?

In the pages that follow, we'll lay out a series of statements that people have made about networking, then we'll ask you to decide whether each statement is a truth or a delusion. As you read on, you'll find that some of our answers are fairly obvious to you; others will surprise you. And some—well, you may find yourself in total disagreement with us, and that's okay. Just look for the kernel of truth. With almost half a century of combined experience in business networking, the three of us have had a lot of hands-on opportunities to tackle these ideas.

You'll find that we often use the terms *networking*, *word of mouth*, and *referral marketing* interchangeably. Don't let this upset you. We know there are subtle but important differences in these three terms, because we have built entire businesses around these principles. However, for purposes of this book, we are using all three terms in the general sense of referral marketing, in which networking is vital and word of mouth plays an important part.

Are you ready? Let's begin with the first "Truth or Delusion?" we ever heard . . .

1. TRUTH OR DELUSION?
Networking is a fad.

DELUSION. Yes, that's right. We're starting with the biggest delusion of all. It wasn't that long ago when businesspeople were saying, "Oh, networking is just the newest craze; it'll never last. You have to get out there and pound the pavement, put up billboards, and place ads in the mass media, the yellow pages, the insides of buses, the outsides of people's shaved heads . . ."

Did you say Truth? Well then, you haven't been paying attention to what's been going on around you. In our lifetime, an entirely new field of study is being codified. Whether you call it networking, word of mouth, referral marketing, relationship marketing, or social capital, it's all about people learning how to connect with other people in meaningful ways despite, or possibly because of, our technological revolution. Geography no longer matters; if you share an interest with someone halfway around the planet, making the connection online is as easy as—no, easier than—picking up the phone and dialing.

And yet, as new as all this technological connectivity is, it simply takes us back to an earlier era, when we lived in small communities with our extended families and knew all our neighbors. We worked for and with people we knew personally. We bought everything we needed from people who were our lifelong friends, were treated for illnesses by doctors who had cared for our parents, and trusted our finances to accountants we saw every week in church.

We don't live in a *Little House on the Prairie* anymore. We

1

don't know our neighbors, and we have very few, if any, relationships with the local business community. When these communities fragmented, much of the community spirit faded as well. No longer did we feel responsibility for the welfare of our friends and neighbors, or that we all shared in the common good. The entire decade of the 1980s was called the "Me Generation," when businesspeople pursued their own interests at the expense of everybody else.

> **Networking is no more a fad than sales and marketing.**

Referral networking arose in the vacuum created by this disappearing sense of community. It has become a way of marketing your business by building the businesses of your fellow networkers. The old ways have become new again. In networking organizations, though we may be lost in a sea of people in our big cities, we form relationships and do business with people who live near us and share a mutual interest in helping our businesses grow. At the same time, our reach is worldwide, giving us vastly more options and resources to tap for any need. It's the best of both worlds—and referral marketing is the discipline that brings it all together.

The first time I was asked, "Isn't this networking thing just a fad?" was in 1987. The question came from a newspaper reporter with one of the largest newspapers in the United States. Confidently I told her, "Networking is no more a fad than sales and marketing." Since I had just started this little networking organization called BNI® (Business Network International), I was hoping that my prediction would prove to be as true as my answer sounded. More than twenty years later, I can confidently say it was. Since that reporter asked me if networking was just a fad, I've written eight books, and my organization has opened thousands of networking groups in dozens of countries across the globe. We have groups speaking almost a dozen different languages, operating on every populated continent of the world. In addition, these groups pass millions of referrals, generating billions of dollars' worth of business for one another. Recently, we've developed a spin-off company (the Referral Institute®), which trains people on something that colleges and universities don't—how to network effectively. In just a few short years, this business has expanded to several countries as well.

Twenty years ago, my instincts told me that I was on to something that would stand the test of time, but I didn't have the body of work behind me that I do now. We truly live in a high-tech, high-touch society. The more technologically advanced we become, the more important it is to reach out and touch real people in our work—to connect on a personal level with people. That is what networking is all about.

—DR. IVAN MISNER

2. TRUTH OR DELUSION?

If you provide good customer service, people will refer business to you.

DELUSION. And here's the reason. Good customer service is a *prerequisite*. It's a minimum expectation.

> Good customer service is a *prerequisite*.

Think about it. Would you refer somebody to me if I provided lousy customer service? Of course not. You'd end up looking like a dope in the eyes of the prospect. Your own credibility would suffer.

Good customer service is part of what the prospect expects when you refer him to me. If you're recommending me to him, I must be something pretty special, right? And if I want to keep that customer coming back, I'll need to give him more than the minimum expectation of simply good customer service; I'll need to provide great, outstanding, memorable customer service to really stand out.

This "Truth or Delusion?" was the genesis for this book. On several occasions, my coauthors and I discussed the point that I made in my book, *The World's Best Known Marketing Secret*, about how people were under the

> delusion that good customer service alone was enough to enable them to build their business through word of mouth. We shared stories about people we'd met over the years who had gone out of business waiting for good word of mouth to rescue them. This got us thinking and talking about all the other delusions people had about networking and referral marketing. Truth or Delusion? We could write a whole book about it. Truth!
>
> —DR. IVAN MISNER

People don't refer you because you meet minimum expectations. They refer you because they expect you to do a good job, which enhances their relationship with the person they are referring. They may not even be doing business with you, so customer service may not be an issue with them personally—but of course they expect you to provide outstanding value to the prospect. They want the prospect to come back to them and say, "Thanks for sending me to Joe Trueblue. He had just what I needed, and the service was great. You sure know some outstanding people!"

Your referral source has a strong interest in making sure everyone comes out a winner. She knows that when the happy customer comes back to you again and again, you're more likely to send business her way when the need arises. The great service you provide to the customer comes back to you in the form of a stronger relationship with your referral partner.

Being in a referral group such as BNI® is one of several important parts of an effective word-of-mouth marketing plan. One of the things these groups emphasize is that you need to be very specific in what you do and in how your product or service is uniquely valuable. If you use general terms, you're at the lowest level of competitive effectiveness. And if you say "customer service," that's not what people are buying.

> We all know of companies and salespeople that couldn't stay in business, despite having superior products. We're also familiar with companies and salespeople that were remarkably successful with just an average product.
>
> Of course, having an excellent product is important. However, technology today has made that common-place and expected. In order to have qualified prospects "beating a path to your door," you must be able to net-work and to market yourself and your product or service in such a way that it makes people want to do business with you and refer you to others. You need to provide them with such a great buying experience that they know they made the right decision. However, to get them there in the first place, it's the networking and marketing that's most important.
>
> —BOB BURG, author of *Endless Referrals*

Don't sell the process; sell the result.

As Ivan points out in his book, *The World's Best Known Marketing Secret*, unhappy customers are eleven times more likely to talk about your business than happy customers. Good customer service only reduces negative word of mouth; it doesn't necessarily increase your business through positive word of mouth.

Don't sell the process; sell the result. Talking about what you do does not motivate people as much as what happens to their client or friend as a result of what you do. I used to sell copiers, and I never met anybody who was buying good customer service. They were buying the ability to make photocopies quickly and reliably. They weren't shopping for customer service, because that's a prerequisite. It's part of what creates that end result.

—MIKE GARRISON

Unhappy customers are eleven times more likely to talk about your business than happy customers.

3. TRUTH OR DELUSION?

If you provide outstanding customer service, and your referral partner has experienced that as a customer, it can definitely increase the number of referrals you receive.

TRUTH. Although good customer service is a prerequisite for cultivating your referral network, great customer service to a referral partner can be a jump start. Referral networks and other referral settings often feature third-party testimonials, in which someone who has used your product or service (in this case, your referral partner) tells the group, "I've used Moe's products, and I'm here to tell you, they're the best I've ever found." Hearing it directly from someone they know is often enough to get people to believe it and act on that belief.

> Never underestimate the power of the third-party testimonial.

I often tell people that testimonials are a very important part of the referral process, especially within referral groups. Never underestimate the power of the third-party testimonial. When you stand up and say, "I've used this person, and you should use this person too, because . . ." and then go on to explain why, it makes a huge difference in how people view that service provider. Your experiences become my experiences. This, of course, makes it much easier for people to refer that provider, even if they haven't personally used his services yet.

—Dr. Ivan Misner

4. TRUTH OR DELUSION?
Word-of-mouth marketing is always working.

TRUTH. It just may not be working in your favor!

You may be thinking, *Hey, I'm not asking anybody to refer me, so word-of-mouth marketing is not something I need to concern myself with. If I provide good products or services, and if my customer service is up to par, I'll naturally get some customers by word of mouth. Why bother with plans and strategies? Why spend all that extra effort to get people to refer me? I'm getting word of mouth free, every day, and it's not costing me any time or effort.*

Well, here's the thing: Yes, you're getting word of mouth every day. It just may not be the kind you're thinking of—the good kind. The message you're sending out may not be clear. It may be too vague. It may even be—surprise!—negative.

Negative? But I have plenty of satisfied customers.

Yes, you probably have lots of satisfied customers, but they're not the ones doing the most talking. You may have ten or one hundred satisfied customers for every one customer who leaves your shop less than happy. But who talks loudest and longest? It's that demanding, unreasonable customer who thinks you're a lousy tailor because you wouldn't take care of her snarling, yapping Cairn Terrier while she went next door to the bakery.

> Yes, you probably have lots of satisfied customers,
> but they're not the ones doing the most talking.

Negative word of mouth has legs. A study conducted in Texas revealed that the average dissatisfied customer gripes to eleven people about his experience, and these eleven in turn tell five others apiece—sixty-six (55 plus the original 11) horror stories about one unhappy trip to your store. Ask yourself: does your average *happy* customer make sure that sixty-six other people hear about your great service? Of course not. Would business be easier if they did? Of course—but they don't. The lesson? Good customer service is important because it reduces negative word of mouth. But by itself, good customer service won't generate enough positive word of mouth to build your business.

Even if you discount the occasional disgruntled ex-customer, your word of mouth may be so vague as to be useless. "Good tailor, eh? What does he do besides alterations? Does he do reweaving? You don't know?" Or it may be misleading. "Well, he has a full lineup of men's clothing, but I don't know whether he does custom tailoring or alterations. It may all be ready-to-wear."

Positive word of mouth that's inaccurate or aimed at the wrong target market may be as detrimental to your business as negative word of mouth. Suppose somebody gets the mistaken idea that you're in the trucking business when you're actually selling trucks. The aggravation of trying to get business done while straightening out an honest misunderstanding may leave enough of a sour taste in the prospect's mouth to cost you future business and referrals. The same is true if your business focus is on high quality but your source promotes you as a low-cost provider. It's important that your marketing message be conveyed accurately and that your prospect knows what to expect. It's a lot easier to exceed the customer's expectations if those expectations are realistic.

So word of mouth is always working. It just may be working against you. If you don't have a strategic plan, then you're not in control of what's being said about you. And if you don't have a way to measure the results of your word-of-mouth marketing, then you have no idea if it's really working.

> **Word of mouth is always working.**
> **It just may be working against you.**

5. TRUTH OR DELUSION?

To be good at networking, you have to be a real "people person."

DELUSION. The only people who can't profit from networking or referral marketing are those who don't like people at all. But these are people who are not likely to be entrepreneurs or involved in sales of some kind in the first place. Most of them will be in careers that allow them to work alone in a back room where they don't have to come in contact with people. They're not going to be out there drumming up business.

Most people who have started their own business and who depend directly on others buying their products or services have at least a certain comfort level in dealing with people. They may not be outgoing or gregarious, but they can form meaningful relationships and communicate their ideas. A lot of people are like that, and for them, referral marketing is the best way to build their business, because referral marketing is marketing through relationships.

Over many years of teaching people the art of networking, we've learned that there are many techniques that can be used to make the process easier—especially for those who are a bit introverted. For example, if you feel uncomfortable walking up to total strangers at a chamber business mixer, you can volunteer to be an ambassador for that group. In this role, you are in effect a host for the chamber, which makes it easier and more natural for you to greet people and say, "Welcome to our event.

My name is _____. I'm an ambassador for the chamber . . ." Before you know it, the ice is broken, and you're engaged in conversation.

It's good advice to remember that a conversation should be a balanced dialogue. It's good to ask questions to get people to talk about themselves, but remember: people who ask too many questions are sometimes perceived as prying, probing busybodies. If you are asking all the questions, there is no exchange, no real conversation, just an interrogation or Q&A. Though most people don't mind a question, even two or three, if you haven't brought something to the banquet of conversation, you can make an "ask" of yourself.

Here's my advice. Read local and national newspapers and a pop-culture blog or *People* magazine. Pick three to five items to use as emergency restarters in case there's a lull in conversation—national news, local topics, sports, fitness, movies, books, hobbies. And food—everybody likes to talk about food. Tell stories about things that have happened to you or to others. People connect with stories, not the factoids and figures of life.

—SUSAN ROANE, author of *How to Work a Room*

Networking is about building relationships. Even introverts (or should we say *especially* introverts) have relationships. The type of networking we recommend can actually be *easier* for the introvert than for the extrovert. The extrovert wants to talk about himself; the introvert wants other people to talk. This is perfect when it comes to building relationships. A good networker has two ears and one mouth and uses them proportionally. A good networker asks questions and gets to know the other person.

> **A good networker has two ears and one mouth and uses them proportionally.**

So if you're introverted, stop using that as an excuse not to network. Introverts who understand this concept are more naturally adept than extroverts at the art of networking because they are comfortable listening to other people, which helps them make true long-term connections with others.

Networking is a skill set that can be learned—no matter your level of gregariousness. If you remain ill at ease in environments where you have to mix and mingle or meet new people, we recommend that you take advantage of some of the many training seminars and workshops that teach you how to network effectively. You'll find that when you learn ways to handle these situations, you'll become more relaxed and confident in a networking setting.

6. TRUTH OR DELUSION?

Practice makes perfect. Practicing networking skills will make you a better networker.

DELUSION. Practice alone is not enough. It must be "good" practice. In martial arts, the *sensei* (master) says, "Perfect practice makes perfect." In other words, if you're just going through the motions, you are *not* learning and growing. Every time you do a *kata* (a system of basic body positioning and movement exercises in karate), you must do it as though you were in a tournament, or as though the sensei were there watching you. Only with that intensity of focus does one improve. The same applies to your networking efforts. If you are applying the techniques halfheartedly, you'll get less-than-acceptable results.

> Practice doesn't make perfect—
> perfect practice makes perfect.

Practicing the skills we talk about in this book is important. But would-be networkers cannot expect to become master networkers by just going through the motions. Take, for instance, the sixty-second presentation or brief commercial you make every week when you attend many types of networking groups or various other organizations. Most people come to the meeting unprepared and unrehearsed, with only a vague idea of what they will talk about. While others give their presentations, instead of listening, they're thinking about how to say what they need to say. When their turn comes, they stumble through an amateurish, marginal presentation. Yes, they practiced, but it was far from perfect practice, and the results prove it.

If you're a teacher, do you wing your lesson plan? The better teachers set goals and objectives for what they want their students to learn. They spend time planning exactly what they are going to cover in class, sometimes down to the exact wording, and they prepare visual aids and handouts that reinforce the subject matter and facilitate learning.

As a businessperson, you should have similar goals and objectives: what, exactly, do you want your listeners to learn about your business that they can pass along to prospects for a possible referral? If you're vague about your lesson plan, if you're unprepared to stand and deliver, your potential referral partners are going to leave the meeting without a clear idea of how to refer you. And you need to practice delivering your message. Standing up and winging it is not going to get you what you want. You have to practice it perfectly if your goal is perfection.

I met a woman years ago who told me she was the consummate networker—hundreds of contacts, a wide-ranging network of people from all walks of life. Then one day in a conversation with me, she dropped a bombshell: she said that her networking efforts weren't paying off for her. She went on at some length about all the groups she went to and people she met and how she made all these contacts but wasn't getting any business. The truth is that she was so busy running around and making appearances that she wasn't learning how to actually *work* the networks and build deep relationships. A music teacher I recently heard about told his students: "Lousy practice makes a lousy musician." The same holds true for networking; lousy networking makes a lousy networker! This is why "practice doesn't make perfect—perfect practice makes perfect."

—DR. IVAN MISNER

7. TRUTH OR DELUSION?
You can't predict referrals.

DELUSION. When you have a fully functioning referral-marketing strategy in operation, you will know approximately how many referrals you can expect, and of what quality, over a given period. True, you won't know exactly whom you're going to be selling to or how much the order will be very far in advance, but that's true of almost all marketing techniques. So if you look at each individual sale, it may be hard to understand exactly how that sales opportunity came to you.

A few years ago, one member of a referral-networking group (we'll call him Frank), a business owner who was well liked and had received plenty of referrals, decided to leave the group. When asked why, Frank explained that the opportunities that had come to him by referral seemed to be random coincidences that had little to do with his networking activities and could never be replicated. Although the members of the referral-networking group liked each other and helped each other whenever they could, he felt that it wasn't working for him the way it should. Anyway, he had been gaining so many new clients that he said he didn't need the group anymore.

When asked to describe a few of the new clients he had acquired, Frank named some individuals who sounded familiar to different members of the group. As it turned out, many of Frank's new clients were people who had come to him through referrals from other members over the past year. But Frank said that it was mostly by chance that he had been introduced to these individuals by members of his group, or by people who knew members of the group. He didn't feel the results were an indication of any system at work; it was just coincidence that his fellow members had bumped into people who just happened to need his services. So why did Frank think these new clients were only coincidental?

Frank's mistake was evaluating his success against the abstract standard of repeatability. His professional training taught him that he and his employees should call people from a list that was generated based on the supposed demographics of his clientele. To generate more business, the theory went, he should call more people.

The clients he got through referrals, on the other hand, always had a story attached to them that couldn't be repeated. This led him to believe the results were coincidental—a misconception that happened because he focused on the individual referral rather than on the relationship that produced the referral.

Referral marketing is like fishing with a net. You're thinking about how to cast the net to optimize your chances of catching fish. You choose a likely spot, you throw your net, and when you pull it in, you find a number of fish. You have a pretty good idea of how many fish you're going to catch if you do this a few times, but you don't know which individual fish are going to end up in your net.

It is no more coincidental that people receive regular and consistent referrals from the people in their network than it is that a fisherman who casts a net catches fish. The fisherman concentrates on his action of casting the net, not the individual path of one of the fishes that swam into it. If he did base his decision on that one random fish, he would quickly come to the same conclusion Frank did: it was coincidental.

> Referral marketing is like fishing with a net . . .
> You have a pretty good idea of how many fish
> you're going to catch if you do this a few times,
> but you don't know which individual fish
> are going to end up in your net.

The reason Frank focused on the referral and not the relationship is because he didn't understand that building effective and profitable relationships is a *system*. In fact, he had never been trained on how to systematically build mutually profitable relationships. In his early training, he was taught about products, customer service, and cold-calling. When he did receive referrals, he had no idea what specific actions he had taken that had caused it—so he was simply thankful for his good luck and went back to what he knew.

When it comes to networking, "luck" is where persistence meets opportunity. There is no coincidence about repeat referrals. It comes from the day-to-day activities of building relationships. Although it can't be measured as easily as tracking cold-call ratios, the results are dramatic and almost never coincidental. Repeat referrals happen because you've laid the groundwork through professional relationships.

What are the odds of that particular five-pound largemouth bass ending up in your net? If you don't know about that fish in advance—what kind of fish it is, how big it is, where it hangs out, what time of day it comes up into the shallows to feed—the odds are pretty low that you'll catch that exact fish. But once you've got it, it's yours.

Like the net fisherman, the referral marketer concentrates not on the individual fish but on the process. He knows the process will bring him many referrals—he just doesn't know who they will be or by what roundabout route they will come to him.

Referral marketing may seem a bit messy and random to those who have been trained to call a list of names in hopes of selling one in a hundred. But it's a system that works well because it is good at ferreting out all those unpredictable, hidden, complex connections that exist between people in everyday life and in business.

Most big companies are still in the dark ages when it comes to networking. The procedures and results are not as easy to measure as cold-calling, so they stick to the old ways when training their sales staff. Someday, savvy people in big companies are going to catch on. When they do, they will create an environment where tracking the progress of a salesperson's networking efforts is important—and they will give their sales departments the time, support, and training to allow that to happen. These systems exist today, but it seems only small businesses are embracing them. When the big guys figure this out—watch out, small companies!

8. TRUTH OR DELUSION?

You can control the amount and frequency with which referrals come to you.

TRUTH. There is a way to make the flow of referrals predictable and adjustable. You and a referral partner can set up a system in which your partner sends you referrals as you need them—regularly, predictably, on request, and on time. Creating such a structured system is like building a pipeline for referrals.

Think about it. What if you knew at all times when a referral partner was going to refer you, to whom she was going to refer you, and how she was going to refer you? What if you knew in advance which product or service your next new customer was going to want to buy? You could plan ahead. You could schedule business to come in when you most needed it and were best able to handle it. You could select the kind of customers you wanted. You could project your cash flow and manage your inventory.

Selling with traditional marketing methods is like fishing with dynamite: you light off a few sticks, throw them into the water, and hope that something comes up. Structured, programmed referral marketing is more like fishing with the latest high-tech gear: you've got a boat that lets you move to where the fish are most likely to be hanging out; you've got sonar that lets you see where the best fish are; and you can say, "Forget those carp over here in the shallows. I'm going to catch those thirty big brown trout down at eighteen feet!"

Yeah, I know it can be said it's like fishing with sonar, but in my mind, programmed referral marketing is more like walking through the forest and selecting which trees to harvest. You don't cut down every one, but you pick the ones you like best. You don't use them all right away. Instead, you create this enormous woodpile—your list of future prospects, all to be provided by your referral partner. You ask for prospects from the woodpile as you need them; your partner keeps control over whether he's actually going to refer them or not. He's not obligated to give up everything he has. But in general, you have a known, preselected reserve of referrals that you know you can access in the future, mostly at a time of your choosing—because *a referral is never an entitlement.*

—MIKE MACEDONIO

How do you build such a structured, predictable referral system? First, you have to establish a close, mutually rewarding relationship of trust with your referral partner. In our program at the Referral Institute®, we've found the best approach is to start off with some relationship-building activities to get to know each other better, based on your behavioral styles and other factors. Next, determine how many and what kind of referrals you will need each week to accomplish your financial sales goal. Then, one by one, you and your counterpart discuss the people in each other's database and identify the ones you'd particularly like to contact. Once this is done, you can decide when, where, and under what circumstances you'd like to meet each one, and if your referral partner agrees, that contact goes into the pipeline.

After contact is made, the results are evaluated and shared with your referral partner. It's about as detailed as you can get with a target market, and the timing couldn't be more precise.

> **A referral is never an entitlement.**

The kind of proactive referral system we're talking about here is not intended for use with everyone you know. It's designed for key relationships you've already formed—that is, relationships of trust in which you and your partner know each other well, along with the level of service each of you provides. The predictability comes from knowing that your partner is a trustworthy and skilled networker who can be relied upon to provide a steady stream of high-quality referrals.

9. TRUTH OR DELUSION?

There is an unlimited supply of referrals.

TRUTH. You may be surprised by this, because most people who are new to referral marketing or who have had trouble getting referrals tend to believe that they must fight hard for a limited supply of good referrals. This mind-set is known as the "scarcity mentality," and those who have it often appear desperate to obtain business—which is not a good way to present yourself when you're trying to sell your products or services. Desperation is not referable.

> **Desperation is not referable.**

It's true that you must compete for business, even within a referral-networking group. When you join a group of this type, you may come in thinking that all the other members will now automatically begin referring all their business to you. What you have to realize, though, is that joining a referral group does not automatically entitle you to referrals; you have to earn them. For starters, you have to work to create relationships where none existed before. Fellow members must get to know you and your work, and they must know that they can trust you to carry out your commitments and to provide outstanding and memorable customer service to anyone they might consider referring to you. They have established relationships of their own, and they don't want to risk those relationships by referring them to someone they don't know.

> A scarcity mentality can lead people to see competitors where there aren't any. There was a fine-dining restaurant I know of that strenuously objected when a donut shop opened up next door. They saw it as direct competition for the same customers: *they serve coffee; we serve coffee.* In reality, there was no competition. Both were food vendors, yes, but that's as far as it went. The donut shop catered to walk-in and take-out customers, mostly in the morning. The fine-dining restaurant served most of its customers their evening meals. It didn't occur to the restaurant owners that the donut shop might even be helping them by bringing new customers into the area, prospects who might not have been aware of its existence. A marketer with an abundance mind-set might have capitalized on the situation by arranging a joint promotion or by encouraging mutual referrals between the two businesses, thereby increasing sales for both.
>
> —MIKE MACEDONIO

But having to compete with established relationships does not cut you off from potential referrals. Suppose, for example, that you're the new chiropractor in your group and you want to get referrals from other members. You learn that one influential member has a long-established relationship with a chiropractor who is not in the group. Does this obligate the other member to stop doing business with her chiropractor and start doing business with you? Of course not, and if you try to make this happen, you will quickly gain a reputation as a relationship assassin—not a good way to be thought of.

If you nurture an abundance mentality, rather than a scarcity mentality, you will realize that there's plenty of business out there for you and many other chiropractors. There is also a way that you can compete and, at the same time, collaborate with another vendor.

First, you know that the other member likes chiropractic. This is a point in your favor, because it means there is a strong chance that she will advise friends and acquaintances to seek chiropractic help as well—perhaps from you, after she gets to know you better. When you talk with her, ask her what the other chiropractor does that she finds especially effective. Does the practitioner specialize in certain therapies?

Ask to be introduced to her chiropractor. Find out what kinds of cases your competitor likes to tackle. Back problems? Joint pain? Neck problems? Tell him that you prefer to special-ize in a different area, and offer to refer cases in his chosen spe-cialty to him. Suggest that the two of you could refer overflow patients to each other and help with each other's patients during vacations.

In other words, you can be genuinely helpful to each other and still be competitors. You can help each other build a cus-tomized practice with the kind of patients you prefer. Suppose he likes accident claims and you don't. You can begin the process by referring a flood of accident business to him—so much of it, in fact, that he may feel the need to send some of his other patients to you.

Even if the other chiropractor and you specialize in the same areas, you can benefit each other by referrals. His practice may be in a completely different part of town from yours. You can collaborate with him in joint screenings at intermediate sites, such as at natural foods co-ops, and give new prospects a choice of chiropractors. Many will choose on the basis of personal rapport, or perhaps the more convenient location.

We recommend Kim George's book *Coaching Into Greatness*. She writes about how a successful, healthy networking activity is what leads to having an abundance mentality. There's a ton of business out there, she points out, and all it takes to cultivate an abundance mentality is to become an active networker, building relationships and providing benefits for your networking partners. Joining a networking group because you expect it to immediately start giving you referrals, without any effort on your part, is lazy networking. It produces few or no referrals and leads you to believe that the number of referrals available is limited—the scarcity mentality.[1]

---

[1]Kim George, *Coaching Into Greatness* (Hoboken, NJ: Wiley, 2006).

10. TRUTH OR DELUSION?
You don't know who they know.

TRUTH. What does this mean? Simply that we don't walk around wearing signs with the names of everyone we know on them. It would probably shock you to learn about some of the influential people your best friend knows but hasn't told you about. You can't assume that your friend, acquaintance, or referral partner doesn't have powerful contacts that can help you, or your business, in important ways.

Never underestimate the depth of the pool that your fellow networkers are swimming in. There's a well-known story among referral networkers about a project management consultant who did business with large manufacturers and was asking for referrals. He was talking with a woman who owned a small gift-basket business, and she expressed interest in helping him. The consultant loftily informed her that he didn't see any possible way she could help him.

> Never underestimate the depth of the pool that
> your fellow networkers are swimming in.

"Well, tell me what you do," she said.

"I go to manufacturers and help them with their processes. I'm sure you've never heard of any of the people I need to meet." He turned and walked away.

The gift-basket woman smiled and said nothing. She had a secret. Among her clients were several large manufacturing companies. She personally knew many executives at higher levels in these companies. Moreover, her father-in-law owned the largest manufacturing company in town. She was the best referral source the consultant could ever have, and he had rudely turned his back and walked away without realizing how much money he had left on the table. She smiled, but she wasn't going to be saying good things about him.

The value that you bring to a referral network or to a strategic alliance is directly related to the number of relationships you have and the quality of those relationships. In a typical referral-networking group of twenty to forty people, the number of referrals that could be created, among all the possible contacts within one or two degrees of separation, is almost incalculable. And it doesn't take a corporate executive to connect you with another corporate executive, or a rich person to introduce you to another rich, influential person. That's not the way the world works anymore, if it ever was.

A friend of ours tells of a high-end property developer who was invited to a networking group's golf tournament as a guest to see what referral networking was all about. He came, but only because he loved golf. As a big-money developer, he "didn't need to network." He came to the awards dinner afterward only because his foursome won.

At the dinner, he happened to be seated next to a financial advisor who had grown wealthy through referral networking and become a property investor. Through conversation, the guest mentioned to the financial advisor that he was having trouble getting a bank loan on a big property deal. Hearing this, the financial advisor told him that he might be interested in investing. Within a few days, the two were negotiating a six-figure deal.

The moral of the story? Always go to dinner. You never know whom you're going to sit next to.

I was in a boardroom with a number of people, discussing whether to form a core group that would grow into a BNI® chapter in southwestern Virginia. I was leading them through some exercises to demonstrate how to create referrals but was not having much success. Frustrated, I said, "All right, let's try this. One at a time, tell us the name of a company you'd like to do business with and the name of the person you'd like to contact. Anybody who knows the person named, raise your hand."

Two of the men in the room were brothers; one was a computer software installer, the other a Realtor. When the software installer's time came, he named a person and said, "I've got this software package that could save this guy a thousand dollars a day, but I don't know anybody who knows him."

At this, his brother jumped up and said, "Why didn't you tell me you wanted to meet that guy? Don't you remember? He was in my wedding! You were there! I play golf with him every week! We're playing today, right after this meeting! Would you like to play golf with him?"

The only way to find out who a person knows is to name names. Not, "Do you know anybody who does such-and-such?" Answering that question requires

> some reflection, and the answer may not jump to mind.
> Instead, ask, "Do you know Joe Blow?" A yes or no
> answer will come back in a split second. Good network-
> ing groups have learned how to use some version of this
> exercise.
>
> —MIKE GARRISON

An associate of ours tells a great story about a financial advisor who received an enormous amount of business referred to
him by a gardener on Cape Cod. Now, how can a gardener be
a primary referral source for a financial advisor? Well, not only
don't you know who they know, you also don't know how well
they know who they know.

> Always go to dinner. You never know whom
> you're going to sit next to.

The gardener was a very upscale gardener who worked at a
number of very big houses owned by some extremely rich people.
He told the investment advisor that he would bring him some
referrals. And the investment advisor thought, *This person can't
possibly help me. He's a digger in the dirt. He's a peon. What leverage, what credibility could this laborer have with his rich bosses?*

Well, the gardener worked all summer long at these big
houses. And who lived in these houses in the summer? The
wives, of course. Who made the decisions about the gardens?
That's right, the wives. So all summer long, the gardener was
developing good professional relationships with the wives.

33

At the end of the summer, the gardener approached one of the wives and said, "Mrs. Gottbucks [not her real name, we hope], can I run something by you? You're pretty affluent, and I imagine you guys have a financial advisor—you know, an expert to help you with your investments. Can I ask you for some advice? See, I've managed to save up a bit of money, and there's this guy in my referral group—who has a really unique way of packaging investments and getting a bigger return—and he says that by using article 32.3(e) in the tax code, I can save a lot on my taxes. He says he's saved dozens of clients thousands of dollars this way. Can you tell me if that sounds right? I suppose your financial advisor is saving you a lot of money that way, right?"

And the wife said, "Gee, I don't know . . . I'll have to check on that. By the way, what did you say your advisor's name is?"

11. TRUTH OR DELUSION?

An accountant is the best center-of-influence referral source for a financial advisor.

DELUSION. The reason we're using the term *center of influence* here is because that is the industry term in the financial services. They are one of the most obvious sources of referrals for investment advisors—which is why they're not necessarily one of the best.

If every financial advisor is taught that she needs to get referrals from an accountant, it automatically creates the most competitive referral relationship on the planet. If every financial advisor is prospecting—and there are a lot more financial advisors than there are accountants—and you are staking your practice, your referral success, on cultivating relationships with one or a few accountants, then you are going after the hardest relationship in the world to create.

An accountant is naturally reluctant to jump into a referral relationship with a financial planner because of the potential of conflict of interest or corrupt intentions on your part. In complex financial holdings, larceny is often easy to conceal; there are many horror stories of people whose accounts have been drained over several months or years by unscrupulous accountants and money managers. Only after an accountant gets to know you well enough to trust you will she risk her client's interests by referring him to a financial planner.

If you do get an opportunity to establish a good working

referral relationship with a sought-after center of influence such as an accountant or an estate-planning attorney, you should guard and nurture that relationship for everything it's worth. But basing your referral strategy exclusively on such formula relationships can come back to bite you. The competition for them is fierce, and you can be in one day and out the next. What's more, your competition may not be only other financial advisors; some accountants are beginning to offer financial advisory services as well, and these will not be inclined to refer you, a competitor, to their clients.

> **The most obvious referral source for your profession may not be the best.**

The bottom line is that, for a financial advisor, an accountant is a good referral source if you can get one, but definitely not the best. It's often better to go after less-obvious referral relationships—such as the gardener.

The larger point here is that the most obvious referral source for your profession may not be the best. Whatever business you are in, there is probably a primary type of referral source that you think is the best possible referral source. If this is the case, stop and examine your assumptions. You may be right in thinking that, as a florist (for example), the local wedding planner is your most likely source of good business. But don't let this blind you to the many other possible referral sources that you've overlooked and that might, if cultivated, bring you far more business.

12. TRUTH OR DELUSION?

You should always get a referral when you're in front of the referral source.

DELUSION! If your strategy requires you to be present in order to get a referral, you're putting severe limits on your potential business. Referrals happen when you're in front of the referral source only if your system is dependent on your asking for the referral and getting it at the same time.

> In a strong, fully functional referral system, most of the referral process is going to happen when you are not present.

In a strong, fully functional referral system, most of the referral process is going to happen when you are not present. You don't want the system to shut down when you're not there; you want your referral partners to be out looking for opportunities to refer you at all times. You want them to be in the habit of recognizing good opportunities for you and persuading prospects to contact you. If they don't think of you when you're out of their sight, you haven't done a good job of training your clients or selling yourself to your referral partners. Which probably means you haven't been doing them much good either.

You should make it your job to equip your referral partners with information about you that can be easily communicated to prospects. You should be making sure they are motivated to refer you when you're not around. And you should have a tracking system that can tell you what happened when you weren't there in person.

> When the occasional face-to-face referral opportunity arises, of course it should not be put off. One time I was at a chamber of commerce event, listening to an insurance agent tell me about the benefits he provides for his clients. He mentioned the name of a person he wanted to meet, a person I happened to know, who owned a large company but was notoriously difficult to get in to see.
>
> I asked the insurance man what it would be worth to him to meet this person. He said, "I'd take you out for dinner!"
>
> "He's standing right behind you," I said. "Come on, I'll introduce you."
>
> I said to the business owner, "This gentleman says he can save you fifty thousand dollars on your premiums this year. Does that interest you enough to want to talk to him right now?" He said yes. The result was a hundred-thousand-dollar referral—and a steak dinner for me.
>
> —MIKE GARRISON

This doesn't mean that you shouldn't ever expect to get referrals when you're present. Sometimes things work out very well under these circumstances. Everybody's had the experience of being introduced to someone at a meeting or a mixer and coming away with a juicy business opportunity in hand. In general, though, you shouldn't limit your referral business to people you've just met. This is known as linear marketing, and it's self-limiting. You can't meet people fast enough to sustain your business and still have time to operate it. Networking is all about leveraging the impact you can have on your target market. If you have others out there promoting and referring you *when you are not present*, your results will be exponential rather than linear.

Avoid turning every gathering into a quest for immediate referrals. If you ask for referrals from a client every time you meet her, you're harming yourself in at least two ways. First, you're training your client or referral partner to refer you when you're there in her face but to forget about you when you're not around. Second, you're just making withdrawals from your relationship bank when you should be making deposits by finding ways to help her. You're giving your partner little or no incentive to refer business to you.

When you're dealing with a client, bringing an expectation of referrals into the meeting sends the client a subtle but destructive message: "I'm going to take care of you, and after I've taken care of you, I'm expecting you to refer me." Or: "Not only do I expect you to pay me, I expect you to refer me." It's better to keep the two transactions separate: one meeting in which your sole purpose is to take care of the customer, another meeting at which you discuss how you can benefit each other's business.

13. TRUTH OR DELUSION?

A director of a nonprofit organization can be one of your best referral sources.

TRUTH. In a typical successful nonprofit, the board of directors is made up of many of the most influential people in the community. The people you meet in and around a nonprofit organization also tend to have a service mind-set. Serving on such a board of directors not only lets you contribute to your community and make deposits in your social capital account, it can bring you opportunities to form high-value friendships and business relationships that can result in high-value referrals.

The executive director of a big nonprofit, such as United Way, typically has a huge network with loads of movers and shakers among their contacts in the business and philanthropic world. Nonprofits need referrals, too, because they depend on donations; and the donors, which are often large corporations, usually have a significant amount of business to give out. Among other services, nonprofits are some of the biggest purchasers of training, coaching, and consulting in the world, because they recruit a lot of nonprofessional volunteers to do their work.

In the state that I live in, Rhode Island, nonprofits are the second-largest industry. A woman I know, who works with one of the local hospitals, told me that most people think of nonprofits simply as fund-raisers for different events. They overlook the many hospitals, universities, insurance entities such as BlueCross BlueShield, and other structured nonprofits that constitute most of the industry. They are significant businesses that need a lot of services. The main difference between a large non-profit and a large profit-making company is that the non-profit doesn't pay a dividend. The nonprofit must reinvest its surplus every year; it stays in the organization, and much of it becomes available for providers of additional products and services.

—MIKE MACEDONIO

14. TRUTH OR DELUSION?

People who like, care, and respect you will refer business to you.

DELUSION! When was the last time you had a referral from your mom? From your dad? From your spouse? Oddly enough, it's often the people most familiar with you who are most casual about giving you referrals. Look at it this way: you've gone out of your way to cultivate your business referral relationships, and you've done so in a largely professional setting, with others who are also interested in getting business referrals. With your family and friends, however, the relationships grow out of non-business, more personal associations; therefore, it may not even occur to a family member to refer business to you—unless you make a point of asking for it.

If you're not in the habit of talking about to whom you're going to refer each other or when and how you're going to refer each other, you'll just continue with that same relationship of liking and trusting each other. It's called inertia.

Familiarity also has its dangers. For example, as much as your mom loves you, she's seen you at your worst—runny-nosed, squalling, tattling, lying, throwing tantrums. Perhaps she secretly harbors the fear that if she referred her best friend to you for business, you'd end up embarrassing her. They know you, they trust you, but they may be hesitant to mix business with personal life. Even more likely, they may not understand *how* to refer you.

In 1987, at the invitation of a local resident named Bill, I went to a rural part of Wyoming to help kick off a new BNI® group for about twenty-five or thirty interested people. He introduced me to the group, and I spent the next hour telling them how networking, and specifically BNI®, worked. Now, by this time I had done about fifty kickoffs in three states, and I had learned to read my audience and recognize when the light went on and they got the concept. Here in No-Man's-Land, Wyoming, on this kickoff morning, I talked and I talked but the light did not go on. They just looked at me with their blank stares.

So I finished my talk and asked if they had any questions. One guy—I'll call him Frank—ignored me but looked over at Bill and drawled, "Bay-ull? What the hay-ull we gotta come here every week for these meetings? Look, man, we got a referral for each other—pick up the phone and call each other. We don't have to come to these dang meetings."

And I thought, *Oh man, I flew five hours to Wyoming to explain how this works, and this guy says why meet, let's just give each other referrals.*

But Bill looked over at the guy and said, "Frank, how long have we known each other?"

Frank said, "Oh, about fifteen years."

"In fifteen years," said Bill, "how many referrals have you given me, Frank?"

"Uh . . . well, I don't think I've given you any."

> "And in fifteen years, how many referrals have I given you?"
>
> "Well, shoot, you ain't given me any either, Bill."
>
> And Bill said, "Frank, that's why we gotta get here every week and go through this because otherwise, you know, we're all a bunch of friends, but we're not helping each other in business."
>
> And just like that, the light went on for not only Frank but the whole group—you could see the spark. Everybody there knew everybody else in the room, they were all friends, and yet none of them had thought to help each other by passing business referrals. Suddenly they understood that it would take a system, a referral-networking group designed to generate referrals, meeting regularly, to get them to do what they could have been doing all along.
>
> —DR. IVAN MISNER

Inexperienced networkers often don't think of seeking referrals except through their customers, which severely limits the number and quality of referrals they will get. Businesspeople who join referral-networking groups expand their horizons, but they still wrongly assume that additional referrals will come only from other group members.

The fact is, anybody can be trained to refer business to you, including friends and family. One of the first things you can do is get them to listen for key words—such as *backache* if you're a chiropractor—and to recognize circumstances where they can, through you, provide a solution to someone's problem.

A lot of research has been done on the reticular activating system. Remember how as soon as you drove your new red Honda Accord off the lot, you started seeing people driving red Honda Accords everywhere you looked—gigantic fleets of red Honda Accords you had never noticed before? That's your reticular activating system at work. You see the things that are relevant to you; you don't see what's not relevant.

Training your referral sources' reticular activating systems to hear the things that are relevant to referrals is key. Even more important is alerting your own reticular activating system to recognize when you have the opportunity to refer one of your referral partners. When you do this, you are cultivating a true referral mind-set in yourself—an awareness that referrals can come from anyone, anywhere, anytime—and you're learning to speak the language of referrals, when appropriate or opportune, in all of your relationships. If you are an unselfish and helpful partner in your outside relationships, others will be happy to reciprocate with business referrals.

My mom is part of my information network. I used to be lazy with her because she would give me referrals I didn't want. Then I said, "Hey, Mom, here's what I could use, and by the way, if you need something, let me know." Now she sends me clippings every week about referral marketing and general marketing and refers business to me that I'm actually interested in. In return, she asks me to refer products and services to her. Instead of taking each other for granted, we help each other out at every opportunity.

Remember the brothers I talked about (page 32), the software technician and the Realtor? They knew, liked, and trusted each other, but it didn't occur to them that they might have valuable referrals for each other.

—MIKE GARRISON

15. TRUTH OR DELUSION?

The majority of business professionals who get involved in referral groups are seasoned, established individuals.

ABSOLUTELY TRUE. A lot of people assume it's the young and the hungry that join referral groups, but the studies don't support that. It's been shown that the ages of referral-group members range from the twenties through the sixties. However, 63 percent of all respondents were forty years old or older. Clearly, this would indicate that the average participant in networking groups are older than some would expect. It's mostly the seasoned business professional who seeks out the long-term benefits of a referral-marketing strategy.

In any good networking organization, selecting qualified members is very important. Good groups tend to select more experienced people over inexperienced ones because they know that seasoned professionals are more likely to bring in an established network. They are also more likely to be good referrals, because experienced people are typically better at what they do for a living. An experienced referral is more likely to work out well and reflect favorably on the person providing the referral.

Note, however, that a good networking group should seek a balance between old pros and newbies. Groups with only seasoned people can be too laid back and easygoing, because most of their members are not in the start-up phase anymore, and no longer are new prospects perceived as being as important to the business as they once were. But a group made up mostly of new people tends to be too frenetic, too hungry.

A good networking group should seek a balance between old pros and newbies.

In well-balanced groups, we've seen very successful partnering between established professionals and younger, newer, "junior" professionals. When the networking veteran takes the newer partner under his wing in a mentoring relationship, coaching her in the finer points of word-of-mouth marketing, the junior professional gains business acumen as she accumulates real-world experience, and both begin to see more referrals coming in. It's a real win-win, Givers Gain® kind of experience: if you give business to others, they will give business to you.

A recent survey of networking group members, conducted by Steve Brewer of St. Thomas University as part of a master's thesis, showed that 74 percent owned their own business. Approximately 40 percent were women, 60 percent men. About one-third of the members were over fifty years old, only 10 percent younger than thirty. The age distribution forms a typical bell curve:

15. TRUTH OR DELUSION?

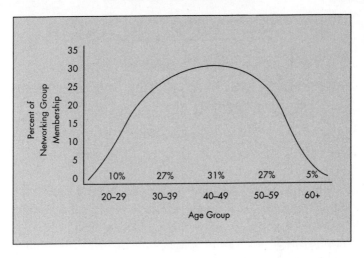

49

16. TRUTH OR DELUSION?

To maximize your chances of getting good referrals, it's best to move from one networking group to another at regular intervals.

DELUSION. That's called "scorched-earth" networking, and it's about as friendly as it sounds. The scorched-earth networker burns and pillages for new business. He's a hunter at business meetings, more interested in bagging the big sale than in building relationships and helping others. He's the old-time "glad-hander" at business mixers, the guy with all the sincerity of Herb Tarlek (the salesman in the old TV show *WKRP in Cincinnati*). He does everything we say *not* to do if you want to build your business through referrals. He represents the absolute worst in networking.

The scorched-earth networker is constantly dissatisfied with the quantity and quality of the referrals he's getting, so he moves on. He flits from one networking group to another, doesn't establish any roots or relationships, networks relentlessly with everyone he meets (often inappropriately), believes that being highly visible is the key to referral success, and expects referrals from others even though he has done nothing that would make anyone else want to help him.

The scorched-earth networker doesn't stay in one place long enough to build the kind of relationships it takes to truly capitalize on referral networking. If he were an apple farmer, he wouldn't be a very good one. He would plant rows of apple trees, and when they didn't mature and bear fruit after only a few days, he would become impatient and start pulling up and replanting the trees in a "better" place. Every time the trees were uprooted, they would grow weaker and weaker, and finally they would die.

The serious networker understands that, in order to build a mature, healthy, and mutually profitable relationship, he must stay where he is and nurture it, and devote a lot of time and effort to growing it. There's plenty of evidence showing that the longer you participate in a networking group, the more business you get. In a study done at the University of San Francisco, Robert Davis found that people who participate in networking groups are above-average networkers. They develop networking skills that the average business professional does not have, and these skills result in more referrals, which means more new clients and higher-quality business.[1]

> The longer you participate in a networking group, the more business you get.

A study I conducted a few years ago (see Dr. Misner's *The World's Best Known Marketing Secret*, chapter 8) showed that people who had been members of a networking group for only one to two years received referrals worth over fifty times as much as the largest referrals received by those who had been members less than a year. The longer members stayed in the networking group, the more referrals they received per year and the more

---

[1]Robert Davis, "A Study of the Relationship Between Networking Skills Inventory Scores and the Quantity and Quality of Leads Exchanged Between Members of the Network" (master's thesis, University of San Francisco, 1991).

valuable, in terms of sales revenue, their referrals became. The likelihood of getting one hundred or more referrals doubles with each year you spend in a business development network. More recent studies done in conjunction with Julien Sharp at Kennedy-Western University support many of these findings.[2]

> **The likelihood of getting one hundred or more referrals doubles with each year you spend in a business development network.**

Have you heard the old saying, "Time equals money"? This is never truer than when it comes to membership in a referral-networking group. The longer you are committed to building the relationships, the greater the results you will experience.

---

[2] Julien Sharp, "Business Referral Study: Replication of 1993 BNI® Study" (Kennedy-Western University, Agora Hills, CA, 2006).

17. TRUTH OR DELUSION?

The best way to ensure referral success is to follow the Golden Rule: treat your referral source the way you want to be treated.

DELUSION. The concept of the Golden Rule (more familiarly, "Do unto others as you would have them do unto you") is a good principle to live by, but it doesn't address what motivates your referral source. All the evidence we've gathered about behavior styles and personal preferences supports what Tony Allessandra calls the Platinum Rule: treat others the way *they* want to be treated. To network effectively, you've got to be relationship based, so you need to use the Platinum Rule—not only with your referral source but with the prospect as well.

> **The Platinum Rule:**
> Treat others the way *they* want to be treated.

There are three people involved in a referral: (1) **Yourself.** You need to know how you work best and where your strengths and weaknesses lie. (2) **The referral source.** How does this person like to communicate? How does he like to be treated? If you want him to help you, you've got to treat him the way he wants to be treated. (3) **The prospect.** How does the prospect like to be sold to? What's the best way to communicate with the prospect?

53

There are a number of different, but similar, systems for evaluating and categorizing personality types. Most make clear distinctions, for example, between fast-paced and slow-paced behavioral styles, as well as between people-oriented and task-oriented individuals. A slow-paced, people-oriented person might want to take her time before introducing you to a prospect; if you try to rush the process, you'll get either no referral or one that's weak, as well as drive away your referral source in the bargain. On the other hand, if a hard-driving, task-oriented source gives you a referral and you hesitate, he may write you off without blinking an eye and hand the opportunity to someone else.

If you understand the behavior styles that people exhibit and you know how to communicate with them, you have a much better chance of getting referrals and closing sales.

One way you can apply this knowledge is by how you show appreciation for a referral, especially when the thank-you is in the form of a personal gift. Dawn Lyons, a BNI® executive director and Referral Institute® franchisee, tells of two gifts she received from two people thanking her for referrals.

One person bought her several items, including a very expensive silk scarf—navy blue, very pricey, clearly of high quality. But Dawn never wore scarves, and she never wore anything that was navy blue. It was frustrating, because the scarf was very nice. It was clear that the woman wanted to show her appreciation for the referral, but she didn't know anything about Dawn.

Dawn's other referral was Mike Macedonio. Mike called a friend of Dawn's and said, "Tell me something about Dawn that I don't know. What's she interested in?" The friend told Mike that Dawn had a passion for all things Greek and had always dreamed of spending a summer in Greece.

Mike went to a bookstore and bought a beautiful, full-color, large-format calendar showing the scenery of Greece, along with a book, a Frommer's guide to Greece. Dawn loved that gift! She hung the calendar above her desk and keeps the book on her coffee table to help her visualize the goal that she wants to achieve.

This is a perfect example of treating people not by the Golden Rule but by the Platinum Rule. The woman who bought the scarf didn't really think about what Dawn would like; she thought about what *she* would like. In fact, Dawn said she could see this woman wearing it because it was her style. But Mike went out of his way to find out what would please Dawn the most.

—Dr. Ivan Misner

Strive to be adaptable. Accommodate the behavioral style of your source when you're working with her, and of your prospect when you've been put in touch with him. Your comfort level is not as important as that of those you are working with. Of course, you can hope that others are as accommodating of your style as you try to be of theirs—especially when you find yourself caught between radically different behavioral styles in your source and your prospect.

By learning about the other person's goals, accomplishments, interests, networks, and skills, you can establish the groundwork for a smooth-running referral relationship from the start. Is she involved in charities? Does she like opera? Does she coach a soccer team? Is she fast paced, or more measured? Does she like to get things done quickly, or is she careful and methodical? When she's talking or making decisions, is she people based, emotionally based, or task based? Look around her office. Does she have trophies and diplomas on the walls, or pictures of family and vacations? All of these factors together will tell you the best way to communicate and what to talk about.

If you seek to find out how people want to be treated, and then treat them that way, you won't make the mistake of assuming everyone likes the same things you do. Looking for a fast way to destroy a budding relationship? Assume that your client or referral partner enjoys deep-sea fishing as avidly as you do and insist he come along on your next *Old Man and the Sea* adventure. Then watch as he turns green and hugs the rail of the boat the entire day.

A woman I know, Rosemarie, who owns an embroidery business, wanted her financial planner to refer her to one of his bigger clients. She kept telling him, "Jim, just say [this, this, and this], then I'll call him, and we'll be all set." Jim would say he wasn't comfortable with that approach and would ask if she had any brochures he could take. She would repeat, "We don't need to do that;

just tell him [this, etc.]." Finally she realized that she was talking to a person with an entirely different communication style and that she wasn't dealing with him the way he wanted to be dealt with. She also realized that the financial advisor knew intuitively that his client might prefer written materials. She said to her financial advisor, "Jim, I'll get you that information." She gave him the brochures, he used them as a lead-in for his client, and she ended up getting the appointment and the job.

—MIKE MACEDONIO

18. TRUTH OR DELUSION?

The person benefiting the most in the referral process is the person receiving the referral.

DELUSION—SOMETIMES. Yes, it's often true that the person who gets the referral is the person who benefits most, because, after all, that's what people join referral networks for, isn't it? You get the opportunity to make a sale to a high-value customer who's more likely to buy from you since someone she knows has recommended you.

But in many cases you could argue that the true winner is the person who provides the referral. In a successful referral, especially in a reciprocal referral relationship, the source walks away with enhanced credibility and a stronger relationship with both the vendor and the customer. Giving a successful referral is one of the best strategies in the world to motivate other people to refer you. If you do it right, you're benefiting not just one relationship but two, and you're creating a third—between the vendor and the customer.

When you receive a referral, your number one responsibility is to make your referral source look good. Closing a sale is good for your bottom line, but enhancing your referral source's relationship with his contact—and therefore with you as well—is worth more to you in the long run. It means your referral source is motivated to keep bringing you business over the long run.

Conversely, the referral giver has the most to lose if the referral turns bad or is handled poorly. The vendor and customer lose the transaction, but for the referral giver, a long-standing relationship, worth far more than a single transaction, is damaged or even destroyed.

> **Your number one responsibility is to make your referral source look good.**

The best of all possible referral situations is a win-win-win: The person receiving the referral wins by getting new business with a potentially valuable customer. The customer wins by getting a superior product or service through a recommendation from the referral giver. And the referral source, although not involved directly in the exchange of money and goods, comes away with an enhanced reputation and credibility. All three parties gain or strengthen relationships of trust.

Another way to look at these relationships is in terms of social capital. Every time you give a successful referral, you're contributing to your own social capital account. Giving a referral to a quality business professional doesn't cost you much time or effort, but it adds significantly to your account with that person if it works out well. This investment can pay off later in a big way, when you may need it most. When it's a win all around, everybody's social capital account is enriched. The networking skills, knowledge, and efforts of all parties are converted into social capital in the form of gratitude, trust, respect, and goodwill.

19. TRUTH OR DELUSION?

Word of mouth is the safest form of advertising.

DELUSION. Word of mouth is the *most effective* form of advertising—but it's not the *safest*. Some people approach referral marketing with the attitude that all they have to do is get to know people and referral business will simply bubble up like water in a spring. What they don't realize is that, once trust evaporates, so does the water.

In word-of-mouth or referral marketing, your integrity and your reputation are on the line all the time. You can't hide behind an ad. In the referral process, you are continually transparent. You've got to do what you say you're going to do. You've got to be professional. Any flaw in your integrity becomes instantly visible to everyone you're dealing with.

> In word-of-mouth or referral marketing, your integrity and your reputation are on the line all the time. You can't hide behind an ad.

When you give a referral, you give away a little bit of your reputation. While giving a good referral will enhance your relationship, a bad referral will hurt it. If the person you referred does a poor job or is dishonest, your reputation is what takes the biggest hit. Your relationship with the prospect will probably suffer, at least temporarily, and you may even lose that person as a customer.

For example, even top-flight master networkers such as ourselves can inadvertently pass a bad referral once in a while. We knew that our company, the Referral Institute®, would be doing a lot of business printing, so Mike A referred one of his clients, who owned a business-printing company, to Mike B. A deal was made, but before long it became apparent that the vendor was charging for services that had not been included in the quote. Mike B called Mike A and complained. Mike A called the business printer and complained. The vendor called Mike B and apologized for neglecting to reveal hidden charges in the contract. Mike B told him, "I'll accept your apology, but I think the bigger apology needs to go to my partner, because he's the one who referred you. You've done him a lot more damage than you've done me."

Since that time, we've done no business with that business printer and would never consider referring him to anyone we know. It was later learned that the vendor had cheated other people that Mike A had referred him to and that, like termites, the damage to Mike A's reputation stayed hidden until it came to light in his own business referral. In the end, Mike A greatly mitigated the damage by contacting and apologizing to each of the people whose business had been harmed by the unscrupulous vendor he had referred them to. In this way, he was able to minimize the damage to his own networking relationships.

As you can see, the biggest risk in this referral was to the referral giver's reputation and business relationships. Many people had hired this printing shyster without a bid process because of Mike A's reputation and clout. This is why referral marketing is dangerous, and it is why the referral provider owes it to himself and others to know as much as possible about the vendor he's referring to others. Take the time to get to know the person you're referring. Make sure that person has integrity, because if he doesn't, your own reputation is at risk. And here's an important point: never give good referrals to people who don't want them or can't handle them with integrity and professionalism.

Similarly, if the person being referred assumes he's got carte blanche because he's a referral, a friend of a friend, he can do himself permanent damage by performing poorly or dishonestly. When your business depends on word of mouth, you can't hide behind a mass advertising campaign and bank on plenty of new customers replacing used-up, disgruntled ones. Word of mouth is always working—if not *for* you, then *against* you.

The same thing goes for the prospect. If you're expecting to get a break—say a special price or a freebie—or if you try to take advantage because a friend referred you to a vendor she knows, there's a strong chance you're damaging the vendor's relationship with the referral giver by making the referral giver look bad. Rather than refer other vendors to you and risk damaging those relationships, chances are the referral giver is going to avoid you in the future.

As you can see, everybody in this three-way referral relationship is in a fishbowl. Everything you're doing or communicating, everything you're displaying is part of your word-of-mouth message. Dishonesty, incompetence, and carelessness quickly become apparent to all. In traditional advertising, a graphic designer can create your image, your brand. In word-of-mouth marketing, your image is not only things that have been created for you but also the way you come to the table—even the way you behave in roles outside of business. If your child's Little League coach is timely, well-behaved, professional, and a good leader, you'll be favorably disposed toward giving him your business when you learn he's also a respected attorney.

> **Remember, word of mouth is always working;**
> **it's just not always working for you.**
> **Especially if you're a jerk.**

Even for someone who is honest, skilled, and dedicated, word-of-mouth marketing may not be the best choice. If your business can ring up plenty of sales based on your customer-service reputation alone, if you are uncomfortable spending the face time needed to maintain good networking relationships, if you don't want to market personally, then traditional advertising should probably be your choice of marketing strategy.

Remember, word of mouth is always working; it's just not always working for you. Especially if you're a jerk.

20. TRUTH OR DELUSION?

If you're getting all the referrals you need, you don't need to sell.

DELUSION. Anybody who's experienced and successful in referral marketing will tell you that sales skills are absolutely required. They're needed in every part of the process—not just in closing the sale with the prospect.

First, you have to sell yourself to your potential referral source—she has to buy the concept that there's value in introducing you to someone she knows. A referral is not a guaranteed sale; it's the opportunity to do business with someone to whom you have been recommended. You still have to close the deal—most of the time. You have to make it clear that you know how to sell, that you can and will provide the products or services you are expected to provide, and that your customer will be happy with both the process and the result—which will reflect favorably on the provider of the referral. If you can't make that first "sale," your potential referral source won't become your referral provider, because she won't be inclined to risk her relationship with the prospect. That is, she won't do her part to sell the referral.

Two separate studies, the one I conducted in the early nineties[1] and the one Sharp conducted in 2006, found that approximately 34 percent of all business referrals turn into sales.

---

[1] Ivan Misner, "Business Development Networks: An Exploratory Study" (PhD diss., University of Southern California, 1993).

This is an outstanding number, but it's still not 100 percent.

Therefore, sales skills are still important in networking. Some people are better at closing sales than others. Having the knowledge and skill to generate the referral, then having the knowledge and skill to close the sale, gives the businessperson a one-two punch.

Second, you have to sell yourself to the prospect in order to get that first appointment. Yes, the referral helps a great deal, but you've still got to convince the prospect that the appointment is worth his time and likely to result in a favorable outcome. You should avoid being aggressive, indecisive, or evasive at this point; the prospect, having been in contact with your referral provider, is expecting a high level of respect and professionalism in your approach. You can and should be confident that a mutually beneficial deal is in the works, and you should communicate this to the prospect by your attitude and actions. Strive not to embarrass your referral source.

Third, once you have made the appointment, you have to persuade the prospect to buy your product or service. This is the part that usually comes to mind when one hears the word *sale*. Your integrity is paramount at this stage. The prospect should know exactly what to expect—no hidden charges, no unexpected exceptions, no bait-and-switch.

If you've created a highly efficient system of generating referrals for your business, you will see a steady stream of referrals being funneled to you. This does not guarantee that you will be capable of closing any of them. You'll need sales skills to turn prospects into new clients, customers, or patients.

Note, however, that in referral marketing, closing the deal with your prospect is neither the beginning nor the end of the selling process. In order to get to this point, you will have made at least two other sales, as noted above. And in order to build and maintain the long-term relationships that characterize referral marketing, you have to follow up with both your new customer and your referral provider—again, part of the total sales process.

Remember, the number one rule in referral marketing is to make your referral provider look good. You need to demonstrate that you know how to sell to the prospect in a way that doesn't embarrass the source of your referral—that you're going to consult with the prospect, discover his needs, offer solutions based on those needs, give him some options, and not force a sale if you know you can't provide a good solution. On the other hand, if your technique is to hold the prospect hostage at his kitchen table until he breaks down and buys, your referral source will not be pleased that you've abused your relationship with him and damaged his relationship with the prospect. You may get the deal, but you've shut yourself off from further deals with that client—and with any future referrals from your source.

The message about sales in referral marketing is this: if you're not comfortable in sales, or if you haven't been professionally trained, sales training is an investment worth your while. It will serve you well in every aspect of relationship marketing and referral networking.

21. TRUTH OR DELUSION?
The more referrals, the better.

DELUSION. Of course it's true that you want to get a good number of referrals, but only up to a point. Taking it to the extreme, you can get as many referrals as you could conceivably handle, but if nearly all of them are of low quality—hard to close or not very valuable when closed—you're no better off than if you simply sat at your desk and spent all day cold-calling. The same is true if you get so many referrals that you can't handle them at the level of quality and professionalism your prospects and your referral sources expect.

At the other extreme, you might get too few referrals to keep your business healthy and growing. You might close a high percentage of them and provide top-notch service, but if you're not getting new referrals, your business may be stagnant and in danger of starving.

Where you want to be is somewhere between these two extremes. You want a decent number of referrals, but not more than you can comfortably handle, and you want to be able to close a good percentage of them for substantial amounts of business. You also need to have the time and the ability to turn marginal referrals into high-quality referrals using your sales skills—and this is something you're not as capable of doing if you're desperate with worry about the number of rejections you're chalking up.

There's a certain psychological illusion that occurs in sales, as well as in referral marketing, that inexperienced or untrained individuals fall prey to. If you get two referrals and your closure rate is 50 percent, that's one sale. If you get ten referrals and have a closure rate of 30 percent, that's three sales. In the first case, you get one refusal; in the second case, you get seven. Even though you're doing three times as much real business, the seven turndowns can create the illusion that you're failing. Being rejected so often can be demoralizing. To compensate, you seek more and more referrals, and your percentage falls even lower.

It takes a certain amount of experience and self-discipline, backed up by a sound measurement system, to limit yourself to exactly the number of referrals you need, at a known and achievable percentage of closure. The self-discipline comes more naturally if you can get referrals to arrive when you need them and when you expect them. A predictable and regular supply of high-quality referrals also helps you raise your closure rate, giving your referral source more confidence in your ability to convert an appointment into a sale.

We know it is possible to create a system that supplies referrals in a reliable, predictable stream, because we've done it. In this system, you develop strategic alliances with referral sources and provide referrals to each other from your database of contacts in an orderly, predictable flow—a virtual pipeline of high-quality referrals. Having control of your referral business—and having a tracking system that tells you exactly how many referrals you're closing over time—is a great confidence booster. If you know that you're going to close 25 percent of your referrals, then you can shrug off the ones you don't close.

A tracking system tells you what each referral is worth to you. Suppose your average sale is worth $1,000. If your overall closing ratio is 25 percent, then one out of every four appointments you get will bring you $1,000. This means that every referral you get is worth $250. So you should treat each referral as a thing of value and show your appreciation to the referral giver, whether you close the sale or not.

It's not about getting more referrals; it's about showing your appreciation for the ones you get and making the most of the opportunity—all the while strengthening your referral relationships to ensure that your referral pipeline flows steadily and reliably.

22. TRUTH OR DELUSION?

One of the advantages of referral marketing is you have people you can blame if things fall through.

DELUSION. One of the misconceptions people sometimes have when they establish a referral network is that, once they've made contact with all these other people who are supposed to start bringing them buckets of referrals, any problems they encounter are usually the result of others not doing their jobs.

The truth? It's all your fault.

"My network's not motivated." Maybe so, but what are you doing to compel them to refer you?

"They don't know my business." What have you done to educate them about what you do?

"They just don't have the contacts I need." You've gone through their entire database of contacts and disqualified every one, right?

It is your obligation to teach your fellow networkers how to refer you. If they're not doing so, then you are not teaching them effectively. So, in the end, it's your fault—or, as a passionate New Age–type business coach once corrected us, "It's your responsibility." And responsibility is something people are sometimes reluctant to take. You're responsible for every action people take on your behalf. It's up to you to choose the right people to have around you, to set the tone for your business, to educate your referral partners about what you do, to demonstrate competence and integrity for those representing you, and to maintain the effectiveness and strength of your referral relationships. If there's a breakdown anywhere in your referral system, it's because there's something you overlooked or let slide.

> It is your obligation to teach your fellow networkers how to refer you. If they're not doing so, then you are not teaching them effectively. So, in the end, it's your fault.

You don't turn over the responsibility to others and then blame them when things don't turn out right; instead, you accept responsibility and work with your partners to ensure that the same mistake doesn't happen twice. You also acknowledge responsibility to anyone who has been wronged, without equivocation. Don't say, "Mistakes were made." Say, "It's my fault that this happened. I apologize for the mistake, and I promise to set things right." This straightforward acceptance of blame has the added benefit of defusing the other person's anger. And it's honest. After all, you created the system that caused the problem. What the injured party wants to hear is acceptance of responsibility and a commitment to correcting the situation—and what the injured party wants to see is action.

One of the strengths of a referral network is that everyone becomes friends. And one of the weaknesses of a referral network is that everyone becomes friends. Only those groups and individuals who recognize that they have to take responsibility, and that there has to be accountability, are the ones who make this process work for them. The people who are constantly blaming someone else for what's going wrong, who are not taking responsibility for changing or fixing it to make it work, will not do well in referral marketing. Remember, if your referral-marketing program is not working—it's all your fault! Okay, for the more tactful among you, it's all your *responsibility*.

> One of the strengths of a referral network
> is that everyone becomes friends.
> And one of the weaknesses of a referral network
> is that everyone becomes friends.

23. TRUTH OR DELUSION?

For networking success, when describing your products or services, you should try to tell people about everything you do.

DELUSION. Don't shotgun your message—sharpshoot it. You may perform a wide variety of services or offer a broad range of products to your customers, but for a referral, your description of what you do should be narrow and detailed, focused on a single aspect of your business. Yes, you may offer the most elaborate assortment of office furnishings available in your part of the state, but that doesn't mean much to the prospect who is looking for a truckload of one specific type of high-tech desk for a new technology company.

> Don't shotgun your message—sharpshoot it.

Your referral sources will find it much easier to get you an appointment with a prospect if you have provided information that will help them address the prospect's specific needs. You're an office-furniture wholesaler? No help. One of your specialties is custom-designed, made-to-order desks, shelves, and file cabinets in large lots? Bingo. You've snagged an appointment.

It seems counterintuitive, but in reality, the more laser-specific you are, the more likely you are to get referrals. People tend to say they "do everything" because they want to catch everyone. They want to throw as broad a net as possible. The problem with a really broad net is that there are big holes in it. When you say, "I'm a full-service printer; I do everything," that doesn't mean anything to your prospects, or to those who refer you to them. What they're thinking is, *I don't need a full-service job. All I need is a particular kind of print job.* If I've come down with a serious illness, it doesn't help me much to know that there are three hospitals in town. What I really want to know is, in which hospital will I find the specialist who can cure me?

> **The more laser-specific you are, the more likely you are to get referrals.**

When you tell a referral partner you're a full-service provider, you're asking her to mentally sort out all the people she knows and cross tabulate what they do against all the things you do. That does not work; people aren't computers. Yes, a referral partner needs to know the full range of products or services that you deal in—eventually. But more immediately, she needs to know with some precision the specific needs you can fulfill, because that is what the customer is focused on in any given instance.

If you say, "Who do you know who is a sports enthusiast? Here's how he can use my product," then you're letting your referral source do a simple, easier kind of mental sorting. The more you can educate people about different things that you do—one at a time—the more likely you are to get referrals in the long run. And getting referrals in a specific area doesn't mean you can't continue to offer other products or services.

When operating in a referral network of some type, your immediate goal is not to close a sale but to train a sales force.

You're training people to refer you, and saying that you're a full-service provider and that you do everything doesn't train anybody at all. You wouldn't tell a salesperson for your company, "Just tell them we do it all." You need to be as specific as possible. As a specialist, you can more easily articulate to your referral sources what you do and how you do it, and they can in turn articulate it more readily to other people. Saying that you "do everything" sounds desperate—as though you have to do it all because you're not successful in any one area.

> Saying that you "do everything" sounds desperate—
> as though you have to do it all because you're
> not successful in any one area.

Someone who professes to be a generalist, who "does everything," is not only less likely to get good referrals, she's also likely to be considered a "relationship assassin" within her referral group. Suppose an insurance agent who's just joined your group comes up to you and says, "I can cover all of your insurance needs. I have life insurance, medical insurance, auto, home, business, and every other kind of insurance you'll ever need. I'd like to be your one-stop insurance shop." But you already have coverage from five or six different agents, most of whom you have solid business and personal relationships with. What she's asking you to do is dump all your relationships and replace them with one relative unknown—herself.

A better approach for her would be to say to you, "I'm a life-insurance agent who specializes in executive benefits, specifically for tradespeople. My passion, in my insurance practice, is to deliver executive-benefits packages to owners and managers of contracting firms so that they're able to retire effectively with tax-protected investments and be able to sell that business." In this way, she's addressing a specific need you may have, but she's not trying to assassinate all of your long-standing relationships. She's presenting herself as an expert in an area where you need expert advice, rather than a generalist with broad but superficial knowledge.

The principle of being specific rather than general also holds true when you're asking for a referral. The more specific you can be, the more likely it is that a person can identify someone who fits the description. If you ask a group of people, "Who do you know who uses art supplies?" you might not get a response; they will think about it and, if no one comes to mind, quickly forget that you asked. On the other hand, if you say, "Who do you know who teaches a first- or second-grade art class?" chances are a name will pop into somebody's head. When you ask me a general question, there are so many different possibilities that I don't even know where to start; but if you narrow it down, then I'm able to sort through the question and pick a couple of alternatives.

—MIKE MACEDONIO

This delusion is really a twofer. There's another delusion hidden inside it: if you present yourself as a specialist, you are limiting your potential referrals and your future business; that is, you can't do business outside your niche. The truth is, whether you're a true specialist or a generalist presenting yourself as a specialist in order to facilitate easy referral, you're not limiting yourself by doing so. People are actually more likely to refer a specialist than a generalist.

If you're like most specialists, although you generally do only one or a few kinds of business, you can still offer many other products or services that are closely related. Yes, you've narrowed down your business to the things you like to do or are able to do best, or that bring you the most profit, but you can do other things as well. And one good way to attract long-term business is by stepping outside your niche and taking on the occasional odd job that can win you a loyal customer for future business.

One last point: if you sell everything, you're not selling on value; you're selling on price. That makes you a provider of commodities. And that strategy can work for you—if you're Wal-Mart.

24. TRUTH OR DELUSION?
Your best source of referrals is your customers.

DELUSION. The reason people sometimes fall into this delusion is that they've been trained to believe it and have never pursued any other source of referrals. The only referrals they've ever received are from customers.

With a well-developed referral network,
you can realize more good referrals from one or two
professional referral sources than from
all your customers combined.

Don't get us wrong. Customers and clients can be a good source of referrals; we know that. However, many businesses (especially big corporations) are out of touch with the fact that other referral sources are available that can be extraordinarily powerful. Clients, although often the most readily available sources, are not necessarily the best or steadiest sources of high-quality referrals. The best sources in the long run are likely to be the people you refer business to. When you help another businessperson build his or her business, you're cultivating a long-term relationship with someone who's motivated to return the favor by bringing business to you, who's sharing your target market, and who will work systematically with you for mutual benefit.

With a well-developed referral network, you can realize more good referrals from one or two professional referral sources than from all your customers combined. Why? Because these professionals are better salespeople than your clients and they spend more time in contact with your target market. They know how to sell to your client base. They talk your talk. If you've done your job of educating and training them to refer business to you, they can communicate your value better to their contacts.

There's also a built-in problem with customers. If you're spending part of your time with a customer trying to get referrals, you're generating a conflict of interest. Instead of devoting all your time and attention to the customer's needs, you're diverting part of that effort toward your own self-interest. The customer may sense that she's not getting full value—and the truth is, she may be right. You may be sending mixed messages. You may be polluting customer service time with "gimme business" time.

Anybody who's in a referral-networking group knows it's not always an either-or thing. A good professional referral source can also be your client. If you use the services of your group's estate-planning attorney, you may regularly and eagerly refer him to others because (1) you know from experience that he's good, and (2) your long-standing personal relationship with him has shown you that he's honest and trustworthy. As both a client and a referral partner, you can be one of his best referral sources.

—MIKE MACEDONIO

Yes, you can expect to get referrals from a happy customer, but you'd better make darn sure the customer is indeed happy. This means keeping your attention—and your motivations—focused on the customer's needs when that is the purpose of the visit or call. However, there's nothing wrong with asking for another appointment specifically so you and your client can discuss how you can help each other.

25. TRUTH OR DELUSION?

Your referral strategy should be customized for each referral source and sales prospect.

TRUTH. As we discussed earlier, always remember the Platinum Rule: treat others the way they want to be treated. This rule applies to every transaction, every relationship you have—with your referral source, with your prospect with your customer, with anybody.

Be aware of the personality types you're dealing with and their behavioral preferences. You've got behavioral preferences of your own, of course, but as the person seeking referrals and asking for a sale, you'll often have to be the one to adapt. In sales, mixed teams of different personality types are often used to cover all the bases and ensure a closer match with the prospect's temperament.

> Your most interesting and productive referrals can come from the most unexpected sources.

Think of yourself as in a partnership with your referral source. If you and your source are of different temperaments, you might be more likely to achieve success if the partner whose personality type more closely matches the prospect's needs takes the lead in asking for an appointment. Face-to-face selling is not your strong point? Better at follow-up? Go to the first meeting with your referral partner, who's a better salesperson.

In any case, you should find out from your source as much as possible about the prospect's preferences before following up on the referral. If you go blind into your first face-to-face, you may find yourself misunderstanding or misconstruing the prospect's needs, responses, and intentions.

The tools and strategies you use will vary over time as well. When you're making your first approach to the prospect, you will use one set of skills. In a growing referral relationship, other skills and strategies will be more productive. And in a mature business relationship, still others will be most appropriate. This applies not only to the development of the relationship but to the age and maturity of your growing business as well as where you and your contacts are in the business cycle.

Even with a full book of business, each year you expect to replace one or a few obsolescent, low-quality client relationships with new, higher-potential ones. In maintaining and using your network, selection of new clients should be part of your strategy, and that strategy depends on the timing for yourself, your referral source, and each prospect.

The secret of successful referral sales—indeed, all sales—is to acquire, develop, and use all the sales tools you can, and learn to match them with the situation and the personality you're dealing with. In referral marketing, the tools include not only your personal and professional skills but also the variety of venues that you can use. Referral masters will urge you to become involved in at least three different kinds of organizations. These usually, but not always, include a strong-contact network such as BNI®, a casual-contact network such as a chamber of commerce, and a charitable or service organization such as the Kiwanis or

Rotary. If you're networking effectively, you'll have occasion to use most or all of these tools because your networks should be as diverse as possible. You should not only seek to network with people like yourself; strive for diversity. Learn to tailor your networking approach for different occasions. Your most interesting and productive referrals can come from the most unexpected sources.

26. TRUTH OR DELUSION?
You can network anywhere, anytime, on any occasion—even at a funeral.

TRUTH. There is no place that's inappropriate for networking. But this is true only if you always remember and follow the number one rule: *honor the event.*

For a master networker, networking is a lifestyle, and it's something that can be incorporated into everything one does. But different events involve very different styles of networking. Networking at a chamber of commerce event is radically different from networking at a church social.

> There is no place that's inappropriate for networking. But this is true only if you always remember and follow the number one rule: *honor the event.*

The first thing to understand is what we mean by *networking.* There's a common misperception that networking is simply using one's connections to sell products or services. This is an understandable error, and it arises because of the way some "networkers" seem to be constantly on the prowl for customers. This is the kind of networker most people can see coming a mile away and try hard to avoid meeting.

In our view, networking is a lifestyle, not a sales tool. It's all about relationships. A true networker is one who constantly seeks to form new relationships and strengthen them by helping others solve problems and achieve goals. It's not a totally unselfish lifestyle, of course; a networker knows that these relationships are two-way relationships that can be drawn upon to help achieve her own goals. But a master networker does not help others with the expectation that every person she helps will immediately reciprocate in kind.

> A true networker is one who constantly seeks to form new relationships and strengthen them by helping others solve problems and achieve goals.

Networking is part of the process of developing social capital. It's similar to a bank account. Every action you take on behalf of someone else builds your social capital account. The larger that account, the higher your expectation of receiving support and assistance when you need it. A substantial social capital account means that you are widely recognized as someone who is generous with his time and energy, who is the go-to person when problems arise, who can be trusted to behave intelligently and honorably.

A few years ago at a black-tie dinner, I found myself seated at a table amid some rather amazing company. On one side of me was the managing partner of an international law firm. Next to him was one of the Beach Boys. On the other side of me was Buzz Aldrin, one of the first two men to walk on the moon, who now is the entrepreneurial founder of the SpaceShare Foundation. Now, how cool was that?

During the course of the evening, Buzz Aldrin and I got to talking. I mentioned that I was working on a new book called *Masters of Success.* Aldrin is certainly a success, and he is passionate about the future of the space program as well. I asked him if he would be interested in sharing his thoughts in this new book, and he agreed to contribute a chapter. The networking I began that evening, although tailored to the event and not aimed at rounding up new business for myself, resulted in mutual benefit for both of us—Aldrin gained visibility for his project, and I gained a prestigious contributor for my book.

—DR. IVAN MISNER

In the widest sense, then, a good networker builds social capital by bringing a Givers Gain® mind-set to every activity she is involved in, to every event that she attends. Her primary motivation is to strengthen her relationships, and this rarely involves thinking, *What can I sell this person?* The event determines which aspects of the relationship are in play.

You would never think of carrying on a business discussion with a networking partner at a solemn social event. However, the fact that you're both attending the event means that you're strengthening the relationship, which will make your business networking relationship stronger in the long run. Everything you do to help another person strengthens your relationship. Look for ways to help at every opportunity.

> What exactly does Givers Gain® mean? It doesn't necessarily mean that if you give you will immediately receive, or that you will receive from the person to whom you gave. It means that if you establish yourself as a source of value to others, and do it consistently, you'll plant so many seeds of goodwill that people will want to have a relationship with you. They may want this relationship because they like dealing with other good people, or perhaps their motivations are simply in their own self-interest. Either reason is valid, providing that the person is of sound character, represents a good product or service, and is someone with whom a mutually beneficial, give-and-take, win-win relationship would serve everybody involved.
>
> —BOB BURG, author of *Endless Referrals*

Can you network at a funeral? It sounds crass, but the answer is yes, if you honor the event. You don't walk around handing out cards, of course, but you offer your help wherever you can see that it is needed. Does a relative of the deceased reveal concerns about inheritance taxes? In a respectful way, offer to call him tomorrow and refer him to a good estate attorney. Does an out-of-town visitor have a flat tire? Call your assistant and ask him to arrange for a quick repair. Seek only to help others; don't even think of gaining advantage for yourself. Your sincerity will be remembered and appreciated.

True networking is the process you use to develop relationships and build your social capital. Therefore, you may network anywhere—but you do so most effectively by honoring the event.

True networking is the process you use to develop relationships and build your social capital. Therefore, you may network anywhere—but you do so most effectively by honoring the event.

27. TRUTH OR DELUSION?

It's not *what* you know, but *who* you know.

DELUSION. It's not *what* you know, or *who* you know—it's *how well you know them* that really counts.

In truth, it begins with who you know because people would rather deal with someone they know, or who is recommended by someone they know, than with someone whose products or services are said to be superior. Even though they know they might find the new items more satisfactory, they feel safer staying with the familiar.

But it's more than who you know. It's how well you know them.

> It's not *what* you know, or *who* you know—
> it's *how well you know them* that really counts.

Here's the difference. Open up your e-mail address book and count the names. How many people do you know? At least that many, probably a lot more.

> All things being equal, people prefer to do business with someone they know and trust. All things *not* being equal, people prefer to do business with someone they know and trust.
>
> —DR. IVAN MISNER

Now, reach into your pocket and pull out your car keys. How many of those people you know would you hand your car keys to?

Most people who are not great networkers concentrate on getting more and more contacts in hopes of finding that one special person who will solve their business needs this month. Master networkers know that a good contact is not necessarily a good connection. In this context, a *contact* is a person you know but with whom you have not yet established a strong relationship; a *connection* is someone who knows you and trusts you because you've taken the time to establish credibility with that person.

In Southern California we have many huge, tall, lush eucalyptus trees that topple over fairly easily in the high winds that occur almost every year. When they're uprooted and blown over, you can see that their root system is broad and wide but not very deep at all. To grow the roots of your network deep, you can do three things:

1. BUILD QUALITY RELATIONSHIPS. Take time beyond normal business interactions to deepen your relationships with referral sources. Invite them to social functions, learn their hobbies and interests, and help them pursue their personal goals.

2. NETWORK IN NEW PLACES. Other than your strong- and casual-contact groups, look for new

areas to find partners with common interests, such as charitable organizations and professional support groups. Don't prospect right away; let the relationships mature.

3. FOCUS ON OTHERS. Rather than having a "What's in it for me?" mind-set, ask yourself, *What can I do for this person?* Continually look for ways to bring business and benefits to others in any group that you're a part of. Make yourself known as the person who always has something for others. This is a powerful way to both deepen and broaden your network.

—DR. IVAN MISNER

Your network must be not only broad but also deep. When you rely on others to cross-market your business or promote your program to a client, you're not asking a simple favor. For true referral networking, you need relationships that are deeper than mere contacts; you need strong connections, established well in advance.

Think of it not as hunting but as farming. Take the time and energy to cultivate deep relationships by giving your referral sources anything and everything you can to help them succeed. These will be relationships you can count on when you need powerful connections. It's not what you know or even who you know—it's how well you know them, how well they know you, and how well they know the people you want to meet.

It's not what you know or even who you know—
it's how well you know them, how well they know
you, and how well they know the people
you want to meet.

28. TRUTH OR DELUSION?

The more networking meetings you go to, the better.

DELUSION. We repeat: referral networking is more about farming than hunting. Running from one networking event to another looking for new relationships is a waste of time, money, and energy that you should be using to develop the relationships you've already started. It's like running around knocking coconuts out of trees when you should be planting coconut trees for the future.

When we train people to network, we surprise them with one of the first things we tell them: Stop networking! Stand still, look at what you have, prioritize it, database it, cull it, and then, rather than continue to work on only the "V" part of the VCP Process™ (visibility, credibility, profitability—see *Business by Referral* by Misner and Davis), devote more time to the "C" and the "P." Credibility comes with a closer, deeper relationship, and profitability is the goal that can be maintained only through constant nurturing of that relationship for mutual benefit. It's not "Nice to meet you; now I've got to go talk to someone over there," it's "How are you doing, and how can I help you achieve your goals?"

One reason that people feel compelled to "Network! Network! Network!" is that there aren't very many sophisticated measurement systems that can tell you how successful a given referral tactic is in getting the results you want. For want of a better system, the "more is better" instinct takes hold, and off you go to yet another networking event. In actuality, all you're doing is adding to your cold-prospecting opportunities and looking for that one big sale.

> **Referral networking is more about farming than hunting.**

The only measurable result of this sort of activity is whether or not you make an immediate sale. It becomes a lottery; for every contact made, it's a hit or, more often, a miss. The long-range success of relationship building is not measured, because it doesn't happen. And yet, that's the real objective of referral networking: you want to develop relationships that will serve as conduits to other customers. The contact that counts, the one you turn into a referral connection by taking the time to develop a mutually beneficial relationship with, may never even buy your product or service. If your focus is the immediate sale, you're going to miss a lot of future opportunities.

The truth is, you can go to too few networking meetings, and you can go to too many. If you're in a strong-contact referral group, you're probably required to show up at the weekly meeting. There's a good reason for this, and it has to do with building and maintaining relationships with your referral partners in the group, keeping up with the different products and services they provide, and being there not only to receive referrals but to pass them to your networking partners as well. But if you make all your required meetings and then proceed to spread yourself too thin by joining and attending a dozen other groups of various kinds, you're quickly going to run out of quality time for your partners.

> I know one couple, a highly successful two-person real-estate operation, that had so much business and developed so many referrals that they had to form a new networking group to find enough people to pass them to. They weren't looking for new referrals for themselves—just enough new people to handle all the business they were bringing to the groups. But unless you are just overwhelmed with business to pass along, I wouldn't recommend doubling up your strong-contact referral networking.
>
> —MIKE GARRISON

You can also spread yourself too thin by getting more referrals than you can manage—in other words, too much of a good thing. Australia's top networking expert Robyn Henderson, who has written *Networking Magic* and many other books on the subject, tells us, "Many people make the mistake of establishing dozens of strategic alliances, forgetting that maintaining these alliances takes time, money, and a lot of energy." Keeping these relationships healthy and productive means meeting your partners regularly and generating lots of good referrals for them—at the peril of neglecting your own core business. Robyn's advice: "Aim for quality, not quantity." Set up your alliances so that you can conduct much of your face-to-face business over the phone or by teleconferencing or video-conferencing. Focus on three alliances in a given year, rank them in importance by your expectations from them, and scale your time on them accordingly. Track and evaluate your results. And don't overcommit. Letting a referral relationship wither from neglect is more damaging than never having formed it in the first place.

29. TRUTH OR DELUSION?

It's best to limit the number and types of networking groups you belong to.

TRUTH. Again, in this case, it's possible to attend too many networking groups, and it's possible to attend too few. The key is to attend a number of different types of groups, and not so many that you have to neglect any of them. Each type is useful in a different way.

If you want something more definitive, we would say that three is the magic number. It can be more or less than three, depending on your abilities and needs, but three is a pretty good target for an effective referral network. You can select from a menu of seven different types:

1. **Strong-contact networks** (referral networking groups such as BNI®) are structured explicitly to pass business referrals among members; they allow only one member per profession. Strong-contact networks are particularly good for developing in-depth relationships because you see the same members week after week and pass referrals as a part of each meeting.

2. **Casual-contact networks** (chambers of commerce, for example) bring businesspeople together in a less-structured context than strong-contact networks, but for many they are a primary source of referrals; membership is

not limited by profession. These groups are good for developing breadth in your network, but deep, long-lasting relationships can be formed as well.

3. **Service organizations** (e.g., Kiwanis, Rotary, Lions, Optimists) are associations that exist to provide and support humanitarian efforts and good works in the community and larger venues. They also bring people together in settings that facilitate referral and knowledge networking. Like casual-contact groups, they help you add breadth and diversity to your network.

4. **Professional associations**, or "knowledge networks," are established to exchange information and ideas among those in a given industry, as well as to promote and support that industry. These networks often include direct competitors, but they also provide contacts in related but no-competing businesses as well.

5. **Social/business organizations**, such as Jaycees or business singles clubs, combine social activities with business networking and can provide a variety of networking opportunities; unfortunately, many tend to resemble singles bars.

6. **Women's networking groups** are still important networking organizations but are slowly disappearing as women enter the business mainstream, especially as professionals, entrepreneurs, and small-business owners. In mixed strong-contact groups such as BNI®, about 40 percent or more of the members are women.

7. **Online networks** are a new phenomenon covering a wide range of interests. Many, such as www.Ecademy.com,

offer business-networking opportunities. Just as with more traditional networking groups, you need to develop relationships of trust with online networks as well. Other ways to network online include starting your own blog and e-mailing your company newsletter.

Not only do we recommend being active in three groups, but we would also suggest that they be three different types of groups. For referral networking, we would suggest that a strong-contact network is particularly important, along with two other groups of different types. If you go to weekly meetings of three groups, you will be spending somewhere between five and six hours per week in meetings, not counting contacts you make outside the meetings in order to follow up on referrals and attend to other group-oriented activities. That's a pretty good investment of time, and if you make full use of your networking groups and develop a fair number of relationships, you will probably have as much business as you can handle.

> **If you make full use of your networking groups and develop a fair number of relationships, you will probably have as much business as you can handle.**

30. TRUTH OR DELUSION?

Unlike cold-calling, the referral process is difficult to measure.

DELUSION. We know this because we've designed a networking scorecard for tracking referrals and the business that results from them. You might want to develop a similar one for your own use. On this card you record the nature and source of each referral, how you followed up on it, how you handled it, how you conducted your networking activities—did you provide your referral source or contact an article of interest? a thank-you note? a phone call? lunch? business?—and the end result of these activities. It's not that hard to analyze what you did and how successful you were in getting business from your referrals.

The referral process is about committing to a series of actions designed to create a result, both for yourself and for the other people involved, and then measuring it and improving the system. As long as you track your activities, it's not that hard to measure the results.

There's a concept we use that's related to the "tipping point" idea for referrals. What's the difference between 211 degrees and 212 degrees? At 211, you just have hot water; at 212, you have boiling water. What can you do with 211-degree water other than make bad coffee and warm up a hot dog? Not too much else. But with 212-degree water, you can make great coffee, sterilize dishes, and start the Industrial Revolution. Can you feel the difference between 211-degree and 212-degree water by sticking your finger in them? Probably not. But one degree makes a world of difference.

A lot of networkers spend a lot of time "warming up" their referral sources, but since they can't tell the difference between someone who is not quite ready to refer and someone who is, they waste time and energy on the wrong person. This is why it is important to have a system in place for measuring actions and their results.

How do you know when you've done enough to get a referral from a potential source? When you track the results, in many instances you will be able to tell what specific action of yours tipped the scales from potential to real results, from warm water to boiling water. Was it your last thank-you note that made a solid referral source out of your contact? Was it that tip on a special deal she could get from a new vendor? You can't measure feelings, but you can discover what made the difference between zero and success. Armed with this knowledge, you can replicate your success at other times and in other settings. In networking, of course, people are different and situations change, but if you track the results under different conditions, you'll begin to see patterns that will show you how to handle your network.

By not tracking results, you're essentially giving up control of your referral networking—which is okay if what you're interested in is shrugging off your own responsibility and finding other people to blame for your failures. If you can't connect success or failure to your own activities, it's easy to say, "This would have worked if my referral source had prepared the prospect," or "The reason I failed is that nobody told me what I needed to know." In reality, your failure to adequately train your referral partners and gather the information you needed to know is directly tied to your failure to set up a way to measure results.

Good referral networking is a lot like luck. Good luck happens to those who have worked hard to prepare for it. If something happens "by chance," such as a good referral, go back and track it. There was probably some series of events, over which you either did or could have had control, that brought you the good luck. Yes, every now and then, for reasons you can't document, you'll get some business out of the blue, but it's hard to write a business plan around that. ("I've got this great business, doing millions of dollars. How do I do it? I don't know. Want to do business with me?") Even a blind squirrel can find a nut! Don't be blind to your referral marketing; make sure to plan this part of your business.

> **Even a blind squirrel can find a nut!**

31. TRUTH OR DELUSION?

Even after you receive a referral, you should put just as much effort into your referral marketing as you did before you received that referral.

TRUTH. There's a phenomenon in sales called *buyer's remorse* that we've all experienced, often from the buyer's side. You've spent a lot of time thinking how great that SUV looks, how much of your stuff it will haul, and how much backcountry exploring you're going to do in it. Then you buy it, and suddenly it is a gas hog, costs a hundred bucks to fill up, and won't fit in your garage. Plus, when are you actually going to have time to drive to Tierra del Fuego anyway?

It's the same product, but once you've made the irrevocable decision to buy it, you begin to regret it. The only thing that's really changed is your attitude. Before the sale, you were focused on the pros—all the reasons why buying would be a good idea. You ignored the cons, the many good reasons that are always there *not* to buy. Only after you'd committed yourself and paid for the product did you start thinking about the cons.

The same is true for someone who gives you a referral. Before she does so, she talks herself into it by concentrating on all the good reasons to do it—her contact will benefit from your services; she will enhance your reputation as someone who can get things done; her relationship with you, her referral partner, will grow stronger—but she ignores the possible downside of referring you to her friend. Once she's passed the referral to you, however, she begins to have doubts. *Is this the product or service my friend actually needs? Will you follow up quickly and deal fairly? Will my friend be happy with the result? Will you be able to make the sale? Will my relationship with either of you suffer? Maybe this referral was a mistake.*

She could, of course, be one of those referral givers who give "good luck" referrals: "Here's the referral, best of luck to you, I'm outta here." But this attitude only leaves the referral giver vulnerable in case the transaction doesn't go well. It may keep her from getting worry lines, but only if she's concerned with just the immediate transaction and not the future of her referral-networking relationships.

Assuming she's a conscientious referral partner and wishes to keep your relationship strong, you need to follow up with her so that she doesn't suffer from referral remorse. As soon as possible after you've made contact with the prospect, inform your source that you've done so, and tell her how things are going. Give her regular updates. Ask her to tell you if the customer is in any way dissatisfied, then handle the problem immediately and cheerfully.

Let your source know how grateful you are for the referral; send a handwritten thank-you note or buy her a nice lunch. Send her a referral fee promptly if that is your understanding, or send an expensive personal gift you know she will like. Look for opportunities to steer business her way. Even if the referral doesn't result in business for you, let her know the circumstances and assure her there are no hard feelings. If she is happy that she gave you the referral, she will be eager to give you more.

Automobile manufacturers want you to be happy with your purchase; they know you'll be thinking about buying another car in a few years, and they want you to come back and buy their brand again. They combat buyer's remorse by continuing to market to you after the sale to remind you of the reasons you bought the vehicle in the first place. They contact you to remind you of warranty-covered services; they conduct owner surveys to show that they're concerned with your satisfaction; they let you know about owners' clubs and special events for your brand. By doing so, they validate your decision and reinforce the positive reasons you had for buying.

As a referral networker, it's in your interest to see that a referral you give works out well for both the buyer and the seller, that they are communicating well, and that both of them are aware of the benefits. Your primary interest is not in making a one-time referral and then cultivating a new relationship to create a new referral but in strengthening your existing relationships so that they will generate many future referrals, both for others and for you.

Now here's the other side of the coin: as the referral receiver, you, too, can experience referral remorse. The business that results from a referral may not be nearly as good as you were led to believe; the prospect may try to skin you because his friend referred you; representations may have been made that you weren't aware of. A conscientious referral giver, aware of this type of referral remorse, will follow up on her own to see how her referral worked out for both of you. After all, if either of you—the referral receiver or the prospect—embarrasses her, that will influence future decisions about referring either one of you. She doesn't want to encourage referral relationships with people who will only weaken her network.

To keep your relationship healthy, tell her right away how the first appointment went, then provide regular updates. If misunderstandings arise, let her be the first to know so she can do her part to repair them. Your forthrightness will reassure her and damp down the fires of her referral remorse; conversely, her interest in the referral and willingness to stay involved will tell you much about her integrity and her concern for others and will influence your own decisions about when and how to refer her to your contacts. Does she care about the referral she just gave you, or is it such a low-level relationship that she doesn't care if you blow it?

> **The work doesn't end after you've passed or received the referral.**

These follow-ups are almost never done, but the few people who do them effectively have a distinct advantage over their competition. They are making sure their relationship with their referral source stays healthy. After all, any referral relationship is a two-way relationship. The work doesn't end after you've passed or received the referral; the way you follow up can make all the difference in the world in how effective your network becomes.

32. TRUTH OR DELUSION?

Your ability to handle referrals from your network is more important than your network's ability to handle referrals from you.

DELUSION. They are equally important.

A true master networker works on building not just her own business but the businesses of her fellow networkers.

If you have a growing customer base, you're going to be generating a lot more business for your referral partners. In order to strengthen your referral network and keep your business growing, you need to make sure your partners can handle all the referrals you will be providing.

> A true master networker works on building not just her own business but the businesses of her fellow networkers.

When you offer your referral partner a business opportunity he can't handle, several things can happen. He may try to provide the product or service but do a poor job, upsetting the customer—your friend or colleague—and damaging your reputation. He may pass the referral along to someone you don't know, taking control of your referral relationship away from you and putting your reputation at risk. Or he may decline the referral, forcing you to spend additional time finding another person to give the referral to. You may have to go outside your network to put the prospect in touch with someone who can get the job done; this defeats the purpose of your referral network. You may even have to admit to your contact that you cannot help him after all.

Referrals work both ways. When you receive one, it benefits your business directly. When you give one, it strengthens your network while benefiting your referral partner. If you grow big and strong but your referral network doesn't, you will eventually become a network of one. To keep this from happening, take every opportunity to enhance your networking partners' businesses; recruit new people and professions to your network; and extend your network through linchpin members that connect you with new industries, professions, and geographic locales.

> If you grow big and strong but your referral network doesn't, you will eventually become a network of one.

33. TRUTH OR DELUSION?

Once you've been referred to someone new, a great way to strengthen your relationship with your new customer is to refer him to someone else.

DELUSION (with a twist). When you accept a referral to a new customer, your number one objective is to make your referral source look good. Your referral source is lending you his credibility and trusting you to do right by the customer, with the expectation that your actions will reflect well on him and enhance his relationship with the contact. So if you take it upon yourself to immediately begin referring your new customer to other people or businesses, it's not your relationship you're putting at risk—after all, that relationship is not even off the ground yet—but your referral giver's relationship with the client. You're taking control of that relationship out of the hands of your source without his participation or permission.

Blindsiding your referral partner in order to jump-start your own relationship with the customer is not a good way to strengthen your existing relationship. This is especially true in the first days and weeks after you've been referred—when referral remorse is most likely to occur. Your actions, no matter how honorable and open, are suspect in these sensitive times, and you don't need to add to the source's worries.

Another thing you absolutely do *not* want to do is hand off a referral. Suppose your referral source—Jack—asks you to get in touch with Fred and offer your coaching services to his staff. You agree, but then your schedule tightens up and you decide, without notifying anybody, to pass along the opportunity to an up-and-coming young coach you've been mentoring, George. George shows up unexpectedly and does a less-than-perfect job. Fred is incensed. Jack is hacked off at you. Your protégé will not be able to do business with either of them anytime soon, if ever at all. Everybody loses.

However, in different circumstances, this delusion can be a truth. Let's say you've followed up on the referral and, after discussing it with the prospect, decided that you are not the right person or business to fulfill the immediate needs of the prospect. Acting with integrity, you may collaborate with your source to refer someone more suitable to the client: "Jack, I know you referred me to your friend Fred, and I thank you, but our conversations have convinced me that Sally could do the job for him better than I could. Maybe the two of us should refer Sally to him. What do you think?"

Time is another factor in turning this delusion into a truth. After some time has passed and your relationship with the customer has endured and grown stronger after several transactions, you may certainly enhance that relationship by referring the customer to different people for needs that neither you nor your original referral source can supply. By this time, you've taken full responsibility for your part of the customer's needs; you haven't replaced your source's relationship with the client, but enhanced it. You've done what you're obliged to do, and now you enhance your relationship with the customer by making referrals of your own. You can refer other providers to the customer, or you can even refer the customer to other prospects whenever suitable, thus creating a new referral partner.

A third exception involves related professions collaborating on a single referral. If you're a real estate agent and Jack refers you to Fred, who wants to buy an office, then it's all right if you refer Fred to a mortgage agent you work with. That's no surprise to anybody, and your referral source would expect you to do it.

34. TRUTH OR DELUSION?

When one of your business relationships passes you a referral, that means the prospect is ready to hear a presentation on your product or service.

DELUSION. Assume nothing. When an associate passes you a referral, say thanks, then start digging for more information. Exactly what does the prospect do? What products or services does he want from you? Will your offerings truly fulfill his needs? What is his behavioral style? What are his business goals? How large is his company?

> Assume nothing. When an associate passes you a referral, say thanks, then start digging for more information.

Don't skip steps in your sales process. Before you approach the prospect, you need to decide on a strategy based on whatever you can find out about him—the same as you would when preparing for any sale. Just because the prospect was referred to you doesn't mean the sale is a done deal. All you've really received is an opportunity to approach the prospect with a favorable introduction. Whether the prospect becomes a client or not depends on how well you convince him that what you offer, at the price and under the conditions that you offer it, will fulfill his needs.

There's quite a bit of difference between a basic referral and one that's well developed, and there are many different levels in between. Listed here from least to most valuable, you should consider which level this referral represents:

- **Name and contact information only.** Unfortunately, this is what many of your potential sources probably think the first time you say the word *referral* to them. It does represent a certain level of trust in you, but the networking value of this kind of referral is low. It's better than nothing—but not much.

- **Authorization to use name.** If he says, "Tell 'em Joe sent you," you can be fairly sure you've established a good level of credibility with him. This gives you some leverage, but the work of developing the prospect still falls on you.

- **Testimonial or letter of introduction.** If your source trusts you enough to say nice things about you, try getting him to go a bit further and write you a letter of introduction or recommendation, including background information on you and some words about your product or service.

- **Introduction call.** A personal phone call on your behalf, preparing the prospect to hear from you, takes significant time and effort in preparation.

- **Letter of introduction and phone call promotion.** A letter that's followed up by a phone call advocating your business represents a high level of commitment by your referral source and has a great deal of influence on the prospect.

- **Meeting.** By arranging and working out the details for a meeting between you and the prospect, your source moves beyond the role of promoter to that of facilitator, or even business agent. This demonstrates to your prospect a deep level of trust in you.

- **Face-to-face introduction and promotion.** Combining an in-person introduction with promotion demonstrates that your source is engaged in selling your product or service rather than just facilitating your sales effort.

- **Closed deal.** Your referral source describes the features and benefits of your product or service, then closes the sale before you even contact the prospect. All you have to do is deliver the goods and collect the money. This is obviously the best kind of referral you can get. To get to this level of referral, you'll have to work with your sources and tell them what you'd like from them. This takes time and education.

The better your source knows you and is confident of your character and your business, the more often you'll get the higher-level referrals. But keep in mind that you need to be making high-level referrals for your sources too. What goes around comes around.

35. TRUTH OR DELUSION?

When you give referrals to others, you can expect them to give you referrals in return.

DELUSION. Referrals are not an entitlement. If you go into a referral relationship expecting that simply giving a referral is enough to get you one in return, you're confusing a relationship with a transaction. In the theory of social capital, the law of reciprocity states that whenever you give, you will get back in abundance. But this is not a simple *quid pro quo*; it's giving benefits, including referrals, to others in order to create and strengthen networking relationships that will, in the long run, bring referrals to you. These referrals may come from anywhere—from someone who knows someone who knows your contact—at some other time, perhaps, from the person himself.

> Referrals are not an entitlement. If you go into a referral relationship expecting that simply giving a referral is enough to get you one in return, you're confusing a relationship with a transaction.

It isn't necessarily that the person whom you referred doesn't want to give you referrals; that person simply may not know anybody who needs what you provide. You can't expect a referral to be manufactured in the absence of somebody's real need. Nor should you expect anybody to refer you if your products or services don't meet their standards. It's your responsibility to meet the necessary standards and to sell others on the fact that you meet those standards. Simply giving a referral is proof of nothing except your good intentions, or perhaps a mercenary expectation that you're entitled to referrals in return.

When it comes to referrals, the law of reciprocity works well *only* if it is not treated as a transactional process. In fact, if the implication to someone is "you owe me one," your actions will be counterproductive. People who feel that you're giving them referrals only to make them beholden to you will avoid you, and you will not be able to form a long-lasting, mutually beneficial relationship.

Choose your relationships wisely. Form relationships with people who are willing to practice the philosophy of giving unconditionally. And remember that, although there is no score-card, when everybody plays by the same rules, everybody wins.

36. TRUTH OR DELUSION?

The larger the networking group, the more referrals it will generate.

TRUTH. True, that is, within each type of referral group. Among strong-contact referral groups, such as BNI®, studies have consistently shown that a group with forty members will typically generate more referrals per member than one with twenty-five members. Among casual-contact networks such as chambers of commerce, a two-hundred-member group will probably generate more referrals than a one-hundred-member group.

This does not imply, however, that a one-hundred-member chamber of commerce will pass more referrals than a forty-member referral-networking organization. The strong-contact group is focused primarily on generating referrals for its members, and it is structured in such a way that time for passing information and referrals is built into each meeting and that members are accountable for generating referrals. A chamber of commerce will offer plenty of opportunities to pass referrals, even some special committees that can serve as a sort of strong-contact referral group, but in general it is not structured to focus on this as a primary activity. Instead, it is part information network, part service organization, and part referral group.

Bear in mind that a master networker does not exclusively need a highly structured organization in order to generate and receive referrals; she can do this in almost any setting because she has highly developed relationship skills. She constantly looks for ways to help or benefit her networking partners, and she has developed a reputation as someone who can get things done, no matter what the organization or situation. For her, a casual-contact group can serve as well as a strong-contact group—perhaps better—because there are more possible connections in a larger group, whether it is structured to make those connections automatically or not. A master networker carries her entire network with her at all times and can make connections that benefit people in different industries, interest groups, and geographic areas who would probably never have heard of each other without her help.

> **Whatever you pay to join a referral-networking group is only the price of admission.**

It's also true that, despite the built-in structure and focus on referrals, a member of a strong-contact group can fail to generate referrals for other members or to receive referrals for himself. Networking skills are the number one requirement; the setting only makes it easier to use these skills. Simply being a member of a strong-contact group does not entitle you to expect or receive referrals. Nor does being a member of a casual-contact group limit the number of referrals you can generate or receive, if you have the skills and use them.

Whatever you pay to join a referral-networking group is only the price of admission—it gets you into the room where opportunities may come your way, but it doesn't entitle you to receive referrals. It's not enough just to show up and participate. You also have to perform.

In other words, if joining a referral-networking group doesn't work out for you, it's all your fault (okay, "your responsibility," for those of you who are more diplomatic).

37. TRUTH OR DELUSION?

Customers generated through referrals have a longer "shelf life."

TRUTH. Studies have shown that customers who come to you by referral do remain customers longer, all else being equal. They come in on a higher relationship level than other customers because they come in on someone else's trust and confidence. The friendship and trust between your prospect and your referral source spills over to include you.

> There is an interesting dynamic among people who look to others for referrals. I have a friend whom others look up to and want to emulate. It's as though by doing business with the same people she does business with, they will become more like her (and that's a good thing because she's a wonderful person). So when she refers someone to her circle of friends, they want to stay with that person as long as she does. If they were "shopping" for the right hair stylist, they might bounce from salon to salon, looking for something better each time, but when they are referred to the hair stylist she uses, they stay with that stylist longer.
>
> —ELISABETH MISNER

Even if you don't make the initial sale, the fact that they were referred often brings customers back for a second shot and a greater likelihood of future business. They'll keep your card and remember it the next time a need for your product or service arises, and they're more likely to refer you to others—all because someone they know and trust recommended you.

38. TRUTH OR DELUSION?

By giving referrals to people, you are also training them to give referrals to others.

DELUSION. If you interact with your clients, customers, referral sources, and contacts with a referral mind-set, show them that you are a giver, help others, and continually and strategically give referrals, you're modeling the behavior you want others to exhibit toward you. By itself, however, that's not enough to train them to give you referrals.

Contacts who are not involved in your strong-contact network may not be aware of what is involved in the kind of true referral networking that you are conducting. Often you will have to coach them as you go, letting them know exactly what you are doing, why you are doing it, and what they may expect from your efforts.

Let's say you've heard about a colleague whose stolen credit cards have been used to run up some big charges: "Stephanie, I've been talking with a colleague about your identity-theft problem and have arranged for him to send you a number of Internet links that will help you quickly straighten out your credit problems. I also know a lawyer who specializes in this field. Would you like for me to contact him for you? I hope you'll keep me updated on your progress, and let me know if there's any other way I can help."

Similarly, if you're passing a referral to an untrained but potentially valuable referral partner, let him know exactly what you're doing and suggest ways he can reciprocate: "Jim, I know a specialist who provides the exact services you say you need. I've known him for fifteen years and have used him many times. He's good, and he's trustworthy. May I ask him to call you? And by the way, if you know a general contractor who constructs steel-frame buildings in the Valley and can use the new kind of fasteners I sell, would you please consider giving me a referral?"

By talking openly about what you're doing, you're not only modeling the behavior you want from your potential referral partner, you're getting him to think about it, which is an essential part of learning. You're also asking him to practice it in a way that will help him repeat the behavior later. It's not a guarantee that he will reciprocate, but it makes it more likely that he will get the idea and respond in kind—at first, out of simple gratitude; later, out of the realization that a continuing referral relationship is good business for both of you.

One of the best ways to train a referral source is to go to a professional referral-training seminar and take your source with you. This way, you will both be trained by an expert and will be speaking the same language—the language of referrals.

39. TRUTH OR DELUSION?

If you join groups and organizations and become active by volunteering, taking on responsibilities, and working side-by-side with other people on a common goal, they will get to know you and refer business to you.

DELUSION. It's easy to think that if you rub elbows with someone long enough, he will spontaneously start sending you business opportunities. That's the entitlement mentality again. But getting referrals usually takes three things: visibility, credibility, and profitability. Ordinary participation in an organization, even a strong-contact referral group, will get you visibility and perhaps some credibility; it won't automatically get you profitability. That takes a much more focused approach, along with some explicit talk about the kinds of referrals you want.

Yes, you're forming relationships, perhaps even rewarding and valuable relationships, but are you forming referral relationships? Not unless you're doing it purposefully and by design. If you're assuming that the idea of giving you referrals is going to pop into someone's head spontaneously if you hang around long enough, you misunderstand the nature of a referral relationship.

Participating in a group is one thing; performing is another. To get referrals, you have to perform. If you don't perform—talk specifics about your business, your specialties, and your ideal referral; and refer business to others in your group—how are they going to know what you do and what you need? You have to take specific actions to let people know how they can refer business to you. Being a good citizen is the right thing to do, but it's not enough to get you the referrals you need to run your business by word-of-mouth marketing.

> If you're assuming that the idea of giving you referrals is going to pop into someone's head spontaneously if you hang around long enough, you misunderstand the nature of a referral relationship.

Woody Allen once said that "90 percent of success is just showing up," but he wasn't talking about referral marketing. "Just showing up" will get you a seat at the table, but you have to pass the food to others and snag your own steak whenever it comes around. It's not "net*sit*" or "net*eat*"—it's "net*work*"! If you want to build your business through referrals, you have to learn how to work the networks to which you belong.

> If you don't attend events, seminars, and programs sponsored by the group, you can consider your membership dues merely a donation. If you only show up and hang back and talk to the people you already know, you don't create visibility.
>
> You have to be seen and heard, you have to volunteer, and you have to contribute your time and expertise in order to create the strong network of colleagues and potential clients that is your safety net. The other members need to know you and know that you are a

competent person with good judgment before they will see you as someone who can do a job they may need or a job they learn about another person's need for.

—SUSAN ROANE, author of *How to Work a Room*

40. TRUTH OR DELUSION?

When evaluating network groups to join, be sure to find one that does not focus exclusively on your target market.

TRUTH. If you choose a group that focuses entirely on your target market, chances are you'll be in a group of people who are a lot like you. Sounds like a good thing, you say? Well, it's not. A group that consists of a whole lot of people like you tends to hang out together in other settings and is likely to have a lot of the same contacts as you. This limits the size of your network, and the diversity as well. It's good to have some people like you in your group, of course, but it's important to have people who are not like you as well. Never assume that someone who is in a totally different industry or social group or market from you can't possibly know anybody you'd like to meet and do business with. You never know who they know.

Even if you share a target market with many others in the group, you can't really tell from the roster or by collecting business cards at the first meeting how effective they will be as referral sources. You have to be in the group for a while before you begin to know who they know and how likely they are to pass along good referrals. Much of this information comes up in open networking before and after the meeting: "Tell me about some of your favorite clients. Who do you like working with and why? What kind of work do you like to do best?" It takes weeks, sometimes months, to develop the kinds of relationships that bear fruit—and until then, you never know who they know.

> Never assume that someone who is in a totally
> different industry or social group or market from
> you can't possibly know anybody you'd like to
> meet and do business with. You never know
> who they know.

Groups that are built primarily on a social model tend to be homogeneous. It's simple human nature for people to cluster in groups according to age, education, income, profession, race, neighborhood, social status, religion, and so forth. Hanging out with similar people makes it easier to carry on conversations, share similar experiences, gossip, and compare notes. It does not tend to expose one to new experiences or new points of view, and it especially does not provide many opportunities to open new frontiers in business or marketing.

We've run across many people over the years who want to form business-to-business networks. They think, *I'm after this market, so therefore I need people just like me all around me.* So who do they get? They get people who are just like themselves. This includes people in businesses that are much like their own and who may not want to share their databases with others. It includes people who have the same kinds of contacts, sometimes even the exact same individuals. Forming a group with such similar people for the purpose of generating referrals is usually a big mistake. (Telling people it's a mistake is a little like telling a boxer,

"Lean into the punch!" It's counterintuitive. Most people don't believe it until you explain why.)

> A few years ago, a rather snooty member of my referral group told me that she had concerns about some of the people in her networking group. I asked her to give me an example. "Well," she said, in a rather sneering tone, "for example, this Amy Smith person—whom does she know?" I looked at her for a minute and then replied, "Well, Julie, she knows you."
>
> —MIKE GARRISON

Networks tend to form naturally among clusters of people who are like each other and who know each other to varying degrees. Your friends tend to be friends with one another. However, if you want a powerful network, you obviously want different contacts and different kinds of contacts. That's why diversity is key in a referral group, and not only in the classic sense of diversity—race, gender, religion, ethnicity—but diversity in types of businesses. We've run into people who didn't want to join a referral network because there was a painting contractor in the group who came to the meeting wearing overalls. But in fact, painting contractors often have great contacts. You never know whose houses they are painting or what kind of connections they've made.

A diversity of personal contacts enables you to include connectors or linchpins in your network—people who have overlapping interests or contacts and can easily and naturally link your group with other, different, clusters of people. These people, according to Wayne Baker in his book *Achieving Success Through Social Capital*, "are the gateways. They create shortcuts across clumps"[1] of people. The strongest networking groups are those that are diverse in many ways; these are the ones that tend to have the most linchpins.

> Diversity is key in a referral group, and not only in the classic sense of diversity—race, gender, religion, ethnicity—but diversity in types of businesses.

Make your network as diverse as possible. Being in contact with a diversity of people gives you access to opportunities you might never have imagined. Networking with a diversity of groups can make *you* a linchpin—a highly favorable position to occupy in any group. People will come to you to broaden their own sphere of contacts and business opportunities. As a go-between and go-to referral source, your value to each of the groups, and to each person in the group, is multiplied. A master networker strives to become a linchpin between as many networks as possible.

Patti Salvucci runs dozens of networking groups for BNI® in the Boston area. One of the groups she visited recently met in a private meeting room at Fenway Park, home of the Boston Red Sox. Arriving early, she saw an older gentleman setting up coffee mugs for the meet-

---

[1]Wayne Baker, *Achieving Success Through Social Capital* (San Francisco, CA: Jossey-Bass, Inc., 2000).

ing. Patti struck up a conversation with the man and was struck by the tenor of his voice. She asked him what he had done before he retired.

He told her he had been a commentator for CNN but had decided to find less hectic work and move closer to his daughter. He now managed the owner's suite at Fenway and enjoyed reminiscing about the famous people he had met while at CNN: John F. Kennedy, Martin Luther King Jr., Nelson Mandela, and others. Patti was astounded.

Later, when the meeting was in full swing, one member, Don, announced that he would like to do a radio talk show someday and was looking for contacts that could help him pursue that dream. After the meeting, Patti directed Don's attention to the gentleman in the back of the room.

"See that guy?" she said.

"The guy who sets up the coffee?" replied Don. "What about him?"

"He used to be a commentator for CNN. Why don't you introduce yourself?"

Don was flabbergasted. It was better than any contact he could have expected, and it happened at the very meeting he asked for it.

The irony was that Don had seen the man on many occasions, but it had never occurred to him to strike up a conversation. After all, the man obviously had little in common with him. What could he possibly have to offer?

—Dr. Ivan Misner

41. TRUTH OR DELUSION?

The more you promote yourself, the more referrals you'll get.

DELUSION. Promoting yourself, in the traditional sense, is not a particularly effective way to get referrals. Just talking about yourself is not enough; you've got to teach people how to refer you. You'd think that people would listen when you describe what you do and then just naturally put two and two together when they come across someone who needs your product or service. But it doesn't often happen that way. People need to be led down the path. You've got to say, "This is what I do. Here's what you need to look for, and this is how you refer me."

Every day we all stand in the middle of a sea of referrals. They are all around us, they happen all the time, but unless we (and our potential referral sources) are trained to pick up on them, we are oblivious to them. The secret is to train yourself and your sources to *listen for the language of referrals*. Tell them, "When someone says, 'I can't,' 'I need,' 'I want,' or 'I don't know,' whatever she says next is a possible referral for me." Teach your sources to listen for words or phrases expressing a specific need: "I can't get this lawnmower engine running right," or "I don't know which tax form I need to use," or "I want to remodel my dining room, but I don't know any good contractors." One of these could translate into a referral for you or someone you know.

Remember also that referral success arises from a system

where information flows in both directions. Approach it not by promoting yourself but by learning about other people's businesses in order to find business for them first. After that you can explain to them what you do—if they're interested. Maintaining a balance, with an emphasis on the philosophy of Givers Gain®, will bring you success in referral marketing.

42. TRUTH OR DELUSION?

In a networking group, you should talk about more than just business.

TRUTH. A referral relationship is much more than just, "I do business, you do business, let's do business." A much better approach is to find common ground on a personal level, then relate your business to it.

The longer we've been involved in networking, the more we've seen the power of personal interests in making connections. Networking is about building personal relationships. If you remove the personal from the equation, you limit the amount of business that can happen. In one networking group we worked with, we introduced an exercise we call the GAINS Exchange, in which people share personal and professional information about themselves. Two of the participants in this group had known each other for more than a year but had never done business. During the exercise, they discovered they both coached their sons' soccer teams. They quickly became close friends and were soon helping each other conduct soccer practices. After a few months, they began referring business to each other—two guys who had barely spoken to each other the first year because they seemed to have so little in common.

Here's another example of the power of mutual personal interests. One of BNI's most instinctive, natural networkers and an avid sailboater, whom we shall call "Bob," found himself sitting in an airport shuttle, very casually dressed, next to a man wearing a shirt with a Nautica label. "Do you sail?" he asked. "Yeah, a little bit," said the man. "Why?"

> **A referral relationship is much more than just, "I do business, you do business, let's do business."**

Bob started talking about his own sailing experiences. It turned out he had won a national championship sailing in the harbor where this man lived. They got into a lively conversation about sailing, the man's hometown, and other common interests and experiences.

After a half hour or so, the man asked, "So, are you a professional sailor?" Bob said, "No, I'm in the training business, but it's a lot like sailing, and here's why." They talked a bit about that, with Bob using sailing as a metaphor for much of what he did. The man expressed an interest in hearing more about it on a professional level. At the airport, the two men exchanged cards and went their separate ways.

If Bob had started the conversation by saying, "I'm a professional trainer," that probably would have been the end of it. Instead, by finding a common interest and starting with that, Bob made a connection that had a good chance of turning into business.

43. TRUTH OR DELUSION?

People are more likely to refer others to you if you give them a finder's fee.

DELUSION. For most referral sources, it is more important to be recognized as a person who can direct others to the goods and services provided by skilled, highly competent, trustworthy people. Most people will do more for simple recognition than for money. However, for those who expect a finder's fee, this is a good thing to know in advance if you want to keep the relationship healthy, active, and profitable.

> **Most people will do more for simple recognition than for money.**

You will find that different motivators will inspire different members of your referral team. This is another area where understanding the various behavioral styles of people can be helpful. People who are embarrassed by being in the spotlight, even for accolades and applause, might prefer their rewards low-key and private—perhaps a simple thank-you or an evening cruise on your yacht. Those who like public recognition might prefer seeing their name showcased on your bulletin board.

Some may be more highly motivated by an inexpensive but thoughtful gift than by a more substantial cash reward. We once met a Realtor in northern California who for many years had offered a one-hundred-dollar finder's fee to anyone who brought him a referral that led to a listing or a sale. This had brought him only a dozen or so referrals. The Realtor lived on a parcel of land that was excellent for growing grapes, so he decided to process his own homegrown vintage wines. He had a graphic artist design a beautiful label for the bottles. Then he told his friends he would not sell his wine but would give away a bottle for each good real-estate referral they brought him.

In half the time he had given away a dozen finder's fees, he awarded a flood of lucrative referrals with dozens of cases of his extraordinary wine—each bottle only costing him less than ten dollars to produce. The personal gift of his wine proved to be a far better incentive than a cash finder's fee with a far higher face value.

A few years ago, I visited my chiropractor for a routine adjustment. Several weeks before, I had referred him to a friend who had recently been in an accident. As I walked into the waiting room, my eyes fell on a bulletin board that was displayed prominently on the wall. The bulletin board read, "We would like to thank the following patients for referring someone to us last month."

Actually, there was nothing unusual about this sign. It had been there on each of my previous visits—but this time, my name was posted on it. I took notice and was pleased, but I didn't give it a second thought, until I returned a month later and saw that my name was no longer on it. Instantly I thought, *Who else can I refer to the doctor so that my name will be put back on the board?*

For the record, I soon came up with another referral for the good doctor.

—DR. IVAN MISNER

44. TRUTH OR DELUSION?

Helping people works. You don't have to have a system for helping people—just help people, and you'll get referrals.

DELUSION. Developing a system for generating referrals is crucial if you expect to be able to rely on them. Going about referral marketing haphazardly will garner haphazard results.

It takes more than just helping people. The people you help have to want your help, know that you're helping, and understand that you did it for them. And real, sustainable success requires that they agree to accept your help and are willing to do the same thing for you. For relationships to last, they have to be mutually beneficial.

This doesn't mean there has to be an equal exchange of services, or business for business. It can be information—how to cut costs, how to be more tolerant of your children, how to cook an omelet without having to clean up the pan, or how to build a prosperous company. It can be support, such as mentoring, a joint promotional program, or a low-interest loan. It can be a powerful referral at just the right time or an influential or personable new contact in your network. All of these are different types of networking activities.

It may seem strange at first to think of designing a system for something that most people consider happy accidents—great referrals—but it's just as necessary and in the long run more rewarding than planning and implementing a traditional marketing strategy. There are several good resources available for developing a strong referral system. We highly recommend *Business by Referral* (Misner and Davis) as a guide.

Replicable systems in business are an important key to success. The funny thing is that most people start pulling systems apart, taking out things they don't want to do, and then they don't understand why the system doesn't work. Imagine a manufacturing production assembly line where someone says, "Oh, let's take this piece off . . . We don't need that . . . Oh, let's remove that part—it's not really necessary . . . Oh, we don't really need that"—then the car rolls off the line, and it's missing tires! Don't let that happen with your referral-marketing system.

We want to make sure that you succeed in your referral-marketing efforts, so raise your right hand and repeat after us (Okay, if someone's in the room with you, just do this in your mind; we don't want anyone to look crazy while they're reading this book). Raise your right hand and say:

"I want to make more money through referrals."

"I promise I will follow a referral-marketing system."

"I want tires on my car!"

45. TRUTH OR DELUSION:

Networking is all about referrals.

TRUTH. It *is* all about referrals—it just may not be all business referrals. Even business networking may not all be about business referrals. It can be sharing ideas, resources, contacts, and information that will help others better run their businesses and achieve success, but it can also be networking to help others improve their personal, social, and spiritual lives. We tend to focus on referral networking because that's the business we're in, but networking is more than just passing referrals for business.

It's important to note that networking takes both a mind-set and a skill set. The mind-set is helping people—the concept of Givers Gain® and the law of reciprocity. The skill set is knowing the appropriate techniques and applying them in the right situations. Just having the right attitude is half the battle—but if you don't apply the skill set, it doesn't matter how good the mind-set is. Conversely, many people acquire a good skill set but fail to develop the right mind-set. As we mentioned earlier, they know how to network, but they develop a reputation as gladhanders, hunters, "scorched-earth" networkers. The relationships they form are not durable, and they have to keep moving, keep hunting. Despite their personal and professional skills, they don't tend to thrive as referral networkers.

46. TRUTH OR DELUSION?

Networking is a uniquely
American phenomenon.

DELUSION. Although the largest referral-networking organization in existence started in Southern California in the 1980s, it has spread to every populated continent on the globe. It has become obvious that referral networking, in particular, takes root and grows quickly in cultures with a large middle class and a tradition of free trade and entrepreneurship.

Networking in its broadest sense is, of course, as old as mankind itself. People have always formed relationships with one another and, through a series of such relationships, exchanged knowledge and resources with people they know and people they never met. The reason referral networking is now becoming a worldwide phenomenon is that it builds on this ancient tradition of person-to-person networking and builds familiarity and trust into a global economy that has, in many cases, broken up the old village economies and forced us to do business with people we don't know and cannot automatically trust.

Our own studies have shown us that referral-networking organizations are growing worldwide simply because people everywhere would rather do business with someone they know or with someone who has been recommended by a friend or colleague. Individuals want referrals; businesses want referrals; the public wants referrals. This is a universal desire, crossing cultural boundaries.

As I have put together business development networks and referral groups in many countries around the world over the last two decades, I have often been told, "That type of networking won't work in this country. We're different." But I have never been discouraged, because the first time I heard this was in Southern California—from people who were only twenty-five miles away from my original group!

Although I didn't realize it at the time, I later came to understand that people who say this are usually people who just don't want to do the hard work necessary to build their referral business. Rather than saying, "I don't want to do that," they find it easier to say, "We're different here."

I have a friend who says things like: "When it comes to ourselves, we're always the exception." "Everybody else should do what's been proven to work, but we're different." "We do things another way." This attitude keeps people from following proven methods of self-development. Only truly successful people understand that everyone who has achieved success has succumbed to the basics. It's the same in business, and it's the same in referral networking.

—DR. IVAN MISNER

Time is needed for relationships to be formed, to mature, and to build mutual trust; therefore, building a referral network takes time. This process must happen in a cultural context, but building relationships is basically the same in all cultures. When it happens within a safe, structured environment, such as an organization that is set up specifically to facilitate networking, then these relationships can form and grow more quickly and easily.

Thus the concept of referral networking can take root and grow in any culture, because the human desire to form relationships is universal. Using networking to help each other's business prosper is a natural extension of our built-in networking capabilities. If the system is applied within the cultural context and not outside it, the same networking concepts and techniques are almost completely transferable from one country to another, no matter the culture, ethnicity, or political persuasion.

No matter how different we are, we all speak the language of referrals. Business is business, no matter where you live. Networking is a great way to *get* business—but it's an even better way to *do* business.

47. TRUTH OR DELUSION?

The number-one trait of master networkers is that they give referrals to others.

DELUSION. According to a survey of more than two thousand businesspeople from four countries that was published in the book *Masters of Networking* (Misner and Morgan), the number one trait of master networkers is that they follow up on the referrals they are given. "Giving referrals" didn't even make the top five!

> The number one trait of master networkers is that they follow up on the referrals they are given.

The reason for this top ranking is that if you present opportunities to someone who consistently fails to follow up successfully—whether it's a simple piece of information, a special contact, or a qualified business referral—it's no secret that you'll eventually stop wasting your time on that person. He's an embarrassment to you, as the referral giver, and to the prospect, who ends up wondering if he did something wrong.

Here are the remaining top-five characteristics of a master networker, according to the survey:

- **Positive attitude.** A consistently negative attitude causes people to dislike you and drives away referrals; a positive attitude makes people want to associate and cooperate with you. Positive business professionals are like magnets. Others want to be around them and will send their friends and family to them.

- **Enthusiasm and motivation.** Think about the people you know. Who gets the most referrals? People who show the most motivation, right? It has been said that the best sales characteristic is enthusiasm. To gain the respect of your fellow networkers, sell yourself with enthusiasm. Once you've done this, your contacts will sell you to others.

- **Trustworthiness.** When you refer one person to another, you put your reputation on the line. You have to be able to trust your referral partner and be trusted in return. Neither you nor anyone else will refer a contact or valuable information to someone who can't be trusted to handle it well.

- **Good listening skills.** Your success as a networker depends on how well you listen and learn. The faster you and your networking partner learn what you need to know about each other, the faster you'll establish a valuable relationship. Communicate well and listen well.

48. TRUTH OR DELUSION?

The best way to follow up with someone you've just met is with a handwritten note.

DELUSION. The best method of follow-up is whatever you actually do—as long as you're consistent.

Come again?

Yes, it sounds a bit lackadaisical, but it's true. Although many networkers will tell you a handwritten note is the most effective way of communicating with a new contact, the truth is that almost any method will work if you use it well and consistently.

When you want to follow up on a new contact—someone you just met, someone you've just been referred to, someone you want to build a solid referral relationship with—the best method is whichever you are most comfortable with and can do every time the need arises. The reason is simple: whatever you do, you've got to do it well, and if you feel obligated to keep doing something that you don't like to do, you won't do it well—at least not consistently. And a late-arriving, clumsy, or half-hearted note in your own messy handwriting is going to make a worse impression than a less "proper" but more heartfelt and immediate telephone call.

Of course, the feeling out there is still that, all things being equal, a handwritten note is best. If you feel this is what you need to do, even though you're lousy at doing it and hate the chore, help is available online at www.SendOutCards.com, a subscription service that makes good follow-up easy. Once you set up an account, all you have to do is go to the site, choose a card type—greeting card, thank-you note, whatever—type in your name, your message, and the name and address of the person you want the note sent to. You can choose a handwriting font, even "sign" it using your own signature. Then you simply hit "Send." The note, which appears handwritten and signed by you, is then printed out off site and mailed in a stamped envelope. It takes only a minute, it looks great, and you don't have to keep a drawer-ful of stamps, note cards, envelopes, and fountain pens.

When I teach management-theory classes in college, students sometimes say to me, "Look, you've just walked me through ten different theories of management. What's the best one to use?" I answer, "The one you consistently apply." Why do I say this? The reason there are different ways of managing people is because people are different. They have different personalities, different approaches, different techniques. And the tried-and-true method that you consistently and effectively apply is the one that's going to work best for you. Follow-up is a similar issue. I know that handwritten notes are considered to be the best way to follow up. The problem is . . . I just don't do them consistently. Therefore, are they really the best technique if you know you're not going to do them regularly? I don't think so. That's why I prefer to *consistently* follow up with an e-mail message, phone call, or better yet, a card using something like the SendOutCards.com system.

—Dr. Ivan Misner

49. TRUTH OR DELUSION?

Reading more about networking will increase your business by referral.

We're going to let you answer this one. You can do it in five stages.

First, to check your understanding of our ideas, read through the following list of Truth or Delusions, which is simply the table of contents from the front of this book. In the blank to the left, check the appropriate blank to indicate whether you believe the statement is a Truth (T) or a Delusion (D). You're on the honor system—no peeking.

Second, after you've taken the test and checked your answers, put a check mark beside the ten Truth or Delusions that resonate most strongly with you—specifically, the top ten things you can do that you've not been doing or could be doing better.

Third, create a plan for how you're going to implement these new ideas into your referral-marketing strategy.

Fourth, devise a simple tracking system that shows the actions you've applied to each referral-networking opportunity and the results of your actions.

Fifth, answer the following question: Did reading *Truth or Delusion?* increase your business by referral? _____ Yes _____ No

If your answer was no, go back to the beginning and read this book again. You missed something.

TRUTH OR DELUSION?

(T = Truth, D = Delusion)

1. ____T _✓_D   Networking is a fad.

2. ____T _✓_D   If you provide good customer service, people will refer business to you.

3. _✓_T ____D   If you provide outstanding customer service and your referral partner has experienced that as a customer, it can definitely increase the number of referrals you receive.

4. _✓_T ____D   Word-of-mouth marketing is always working.

5. _✓_T ____D   To be good at networking, you have to be a real "people person."

6. _✓_T ____D   Practice makes perfect. Practicing networking skills will make you a better networker.

7. _✓_T ____D   You can't predict referrals.

8. ____T _✓_D   You can control the amount and frequency with which referrals come to you.

9. _✓_T ____D   There is an unlimited supply of referrals.

10. _✓_T ____D   You don't know who they know.

11. ____T _✓_D   An accountant is the best center-of-influence referral source for a financial advisor.

12. _✓_T ____D   You should always get a referral when you're in front of the referral source.

13. ____T _✓_D   A director of a nonprofit organization can be one of your best referral sources.

14. _____T __✓__D   People who like, care, and respect you will refer business to you.

15. __✓__T _____D   The majority of business professionals who get involved in referral groups are seasoned, established individuals.

16. _____T __✓__D   To maximize your chances of getting good referrals, it's best to move from one networking group to another at regular intervals.

17. _____T __✓__D   The best way to ensure referral success is to follow the Golden Rule: treat your referral source the way you want to be treated.

18. _____T __✓__D   The person benefiting the most in the referral process is the person receiving the referral.

19. _____T __✓__D   Word of mouth is the safest form of advertising.

20. _____T __✓__D   If you're getting all the referrals you need, you don't need to sell.

21. __✓__T _____D   The more referrals, the better.

22. _____T __✓__D   One of the advantages of referral marketing is you have people you can blame if things fall through.

23. _____T __✓__D   For networking success, when describing your products or services, you should try to tell people about everything you do.

24. _____T __✓__D   Your best source of referrals is your customers.

25. __✓__T _____D   Your referral strategy should be

customized for each referral source and sales prospect.

26. _____T _____D You can network anywhere, anytime, on any occasion—even at a funeral.

27. _____T _____D It's not *what* you know, but *who* you know.

28. _____T _____D The more networking meetings you go to, the better.

29. _____T _____D It's best to limit the number and types of networking groups you belong to.

30. _____T _____D Unlike cold-calling, the referral process is difficult to measure.

31. _____T _____D Even after you receive a referral, you should put just as much effort into your referral marketing as you did before you received that referral.

32. _____T _____D Your ability to handle referrals from your network is more important than your network's ability to handle referrals from you.

33. _____T _____D Once you've been referred to someone new, a great way to strengthen your relationship with your new customer is to refer him to someone else.

34. _____T _____D When one of your business relationships passes you a referral, that means the prospect is ready to hear a presentation on your product or service.

35. _____T _____D When you give referrals to others, you can expect them to give you referrals in return.

36. _____T _____D   The larger the networking group, the more referrals it will generate.

37. _____T _____D   Customers generated through referrals have a longer "shelf life."

38. _____T _____D   By giving referrals to people, you are also training them to give referrals to others.

39. _____T _____D   If you join groups and organizations and become active by volunteering, taking on responsibilities, and working side-by-side with other people on a common goal, they will get to know you and refer business to you.

40. _____T _____D   When evaluating network groups to join, be sure to find one that does not focus exclusively on your target market.

41. _____T _____D   The more you promote yourself, the more referrals you'll get.

42. _____T _____D   In a networking group, you should talk about more than just business.

43. _____T _____D   People are more likely to refer others to you if you give them a finder's fee.

44. _____T _____D   Helping people works. You don't have to have a system for helping people— just help people, and you'll get referrals.

45. _____T _____D   Networking is all about referrals.

46. _____T _____D   Networking is a uniquely American phenomenon.

47. _____T _____D   The number-one trait of master networkers is that they give referrals to others.

48. _____T _____D   The best way to follow up with someone you've just met is with a handwritten note.

49. _____T _____D   Reading more about networking will increase your business by referral.

All the answers can be found on the following page.

NOTE TO THE READER: If you've finished this book and you feel there is a "Truth or Delusion" missing, let us know by e-mailing us at info@TruthorDelusion.com. We'd like to hear your comments.

—The Authors

KEY TO
TRUTH OR DELUSION? QUIZ

1. D	26. T
2. D	27. D
3. T	28. D
4. T	29. T
5. D	30. D
6. D	31. T
7. D	32. D
8. T	33. D (T)
9. T	34. D
10. T	35. D
11. D	36. T
12. D	37. T
13. T	38. D
14. D	39. D
15. T	40. T
16. D	41. D
17. D	42. T
18. D	43. D
19. D	44. D
20. D	45. T
21. D	46. D
22. D	47. D
23. D	48. D
24. D	49. Your call!
25. T	

ACKNOWLEDGMENTS

For years we've been running into networkers who tell us, "You know, a lot of people think referral networking is like this, but it's really like that." We found that most of these folks had given their ideas a lot of thought and had come to correct, and useful, insights.

As trainers, we are also aware that people who are new to networking often come into it with untrue assumptions or pick up mistaken notions about it from people who haven't mastered it. To truly understand networking and become masters of referrals, they need to learn which ideas are true and which are delusional.

We have kept an ever-growing journal of "facts" about networking that sometimes lead referral networkers off in the wrong direction. To these we've added an ever-growing list of comments from our fellow networkers. When the time drew near to turn this compilation into a book, we called and wrote other friends, colleagues, and networking masters and asked them for their ideas to make the book as comprehensive and useful as possible. Because we are reasonably sure that the book does not yet cover all the possible misconceptions of networking, we invite readers to contact us and add their own, which could end up in a second edition or even a sequel.

For their generous contributions to the writing of this book, we are grateful to Brian Alcorn, Beth Anderson, Susan Bean, Beverley Blandford, Bob Burg, Patrick Carney, Victor Clarke, Denis Brisson and Jocelyne D'Aoustim, Norm Dominguez,

ACKNOWLEDGMENTS

Eddie Esposito, Tom Fleming, Paula Frazier, Jocelyn Garrison, Kim George, Dan and Penny Georgevich, Patrick Guiden, Jason Hager, Robyn Henderson, Dick Herron, Connie Hinton, Tim Houston, Dani Johnson, Hugh Lee, Dawn Lyons, Linda Macedonio, Brett Malofsky, Trey McAllister, Beth Misner, Ed Owen, Sarah Owen, Emile Paradis, Susan RoAne, Michael Roberts, Patty Salvucci, Deanna Schmitt, Gunnar Selheden, Scott Simon, Robert Steffen, Jenn Taggart, and Dr. Garrett Thompson.

ABOUT THE AUTHORS

IVAN R. MISNER, PHD, is the founder and chairman of BNI® (Business Network International), the largest business-networking organization in the world. Founded in 1985, BNI® now has thousands of chapters throughout every populated continent of the world. Each year, BNI® generates millions of referrals resulting in billions of dollars' worth of business for its members.

Dr. Misner's doctoral degree is from the University of Southern California. He has written nine books, including the *New York Times* best seller *Masters of Networking* and his number one bestseller *Masters of Success*. He is a monthly columnist for Entrepreneur.com and is chairman of the board of the Referral Institute®, a referral-training company with trainers around the world. He has taught business and social capital courses at several universities and sits on the board of directors for the Colorado School of Professional Psychology.

Called the "Father of Modern Networking" by Ecademy.com and the "Networking Guru" by *Entrepreneur* magazine, Dr. Misner is one of the world's leading experts on business networking and has been a keynote speaker for major corporations and associations throughout the world. He has been featured in the *Los Angeles Times, Wall Street Journal,* and *New York Times,* as well as numerous television and radio shows on networks such as CNN, CNBC, and the BBC in London.

Dr. Misner serves on the board of directors for the Haynes Children Center. He is the founder of the BNI-Misner Charitable Foundation and was recently named Humanitarian of the Year by the *Daily Bulletin.* He is married and lives with his wife, Elisabeth, and their three children in Claremont, California. In his spare time (!), he is also an amateur magician and holds a black belt in karate.

MICHAEL MACEDONIO spent more than twenty years in restaurant management, including managing the highest-volume restaurant in the nation. As part owner of several BNI® franchises, he trained business professionals how to create and operate professional business-referral groups. During his nine years with BNI®, Michael was involved in building his region to more than seventy chapters with more than fifteen hundred members in three states. He also received numerous national awards from BNI®, including the National Director of the Year Award.

Michael's great passions are mountain climbing, cycling, and endurance sports. He has completed numerous marathons, biathlons, and triathlons, and in June 2005 he summitted Mt. Rainier in Washington State.

In 2001, Michael became a trainer at the Referral Institute®, where he focused on consulting with and coaching individuals and companies on how to build their business by utilizing referral strategies. In 2003, Michael was hand selected to be the managing partner for the Referral Institute®. Since then, the Referral Institute® has grown from a handful of professional trainers, collaborating and working together, to a franchised organization. In fact, Michael was responsible for spearheading the acquisition of thirty-five new franchises in six different countries in just eighteen months.

Today, as president of the Referral Institute®, Michael works directly with his franchisees and is responsible for showing them a results-orientated system for building their training and coaching businesses. Ultimately, Michael is confident that the training programs offered by the Referral Institute® will allow his franchisees worldwide to provide new and effective ways for local business owners to create more business by referral. Michael has three major goals for the Referral Institute®: (1) to have extremely successful franchise owners, (2) to have extremely successful local business professionals in each franchise who have implemented the training materials and created documented success from the programs, and (3) to develop the Referral Institute® into "The World's Leading Referral Training Organization"!

MICHAEL J. GARRISON (Mike to his friends) is vice president of the Referral Institute®. For over a decade Mike was directly associated with BNI®, the world's largest referral organization, leading multiple award-winning franchises in diverse markets in the United States. He credits BNI® as the premier environment in the world to develop real-world networking experience on a weekly basis.

Mike is a sought-after speaker, coach, and consultant on business networking, referral marketing, and Christian business topics. He has spoken internationally and cannot wait for his next opportunity to both share and experience how other cultures develop effective business relationships that produce results. He is proud to be a contributing author to the number one bestseller *Masters of Success*.

Mike, his wife, Jocelyn, and their son, Robert, live in Roanoke, Virginia. He loves living in the Blue Ridge Mountains and spends many hours outside playing golf, mountain biking, and hiking. Mike reads as much as he can about business, history, and religion. He credits his success to his faith and to the relationships that God has blessed him with.

REFERRAL®
INSTITUTE

The Referral Institute® is one of the leading referral-training organizations with franchises, trainers, and coaches around the world. The organization teaches business professionals how to harness the power of referral marketing to drive sales for long-term, sustainable business growth by referral. Founded in 2001, the Referral Institute® began developing training materials specific to referral marketing. Today, the Referral Institute® is a franchised company. Its three partners—senior partner Dr. Ivan Misner, president Mike Macedonio, and vice president Mike Garrison—are proud to announce that Entrepreneur.com noticed how quickly the Referral Institute® was growing and recognized it as one of the top five hundred franchised companies in the world.

The Referral Institute's mission is to direct professionals to proactively increase their business through implementing structured referral strategies. In total, the Referral Institute® provides the world's leading material on referral marketing in three different areas:

Referral-Marketing Training. The Referral Institute® offers students one-day programs, as well as programs covering several modules over ten to twelve weeks. The Pipeline Program™, our signature class, requires participants to attend the class with a referral source. The one-day Pipeline Seminar teaches a simple, highly manageable referral process in which participants leave the training having scheduled appointments with qualified prospects.

Another popular program is our Understanding GEMS™ program. This one-day program teaches how your behavioral style affects your referability. Students participate in a behavioral assessment, are taught how to recognize behavioral styles and adapt to them, and learn how to work with and develop referral sources. Students realize that each behavioral style is truly a "Gem" to work with, *if* you know how!

Our ten- to twelve-week course is called *Certified Networker*™. This course is truly a foundational course for understanding, developing, and tracking your referral business. In most cases, Certified Networker™ will simply change the way that business owners do business. It narrows their target market, provides them with mission statements, and shows them how profitable it can be to develop referral sources by being strategic. Certified Networker™ is a must for anyone new to referral marketing.

Referral-Marketing Coaching. As students of the Referral Institute® begin learning the formulas and philosophies necessary to implement referral marketing, they are also encouraged to have accountability. Our coaches have received intense training on behavioral styles and referral-marketing plans, and they are required to graduate from our Directive Coaching School. Being coached by a Referral Institute® coach will ensure your success in creating the long-term referral sources that bring you more business by referral.

Referral-Marketing Consulting. Our consultants will design and implement customized referral-marketing plans with businesses and corporate clients. Combining training, coaching, and collaboration, our consultants are able to tailor the Referral

Institute's programs to work with one employee or hundreds of employees around the world. This is the ultimate process for integrating referral marketing into your business or your corporate culture.

Please browse our Web site at www.referralinstitute.com to learn more about referral marketing, as well as how to attend a Referral Institute® training program in your area. You may also contact the president, Mike Macedonio, at mikem@ referralinstitute.com to talk about growing your business by generating qualified referrals.

BNI®

BNI® (Business Network International) was founded by Dr. Ivan Misner in 1985 as a way for businesspeople to generate referrals in a structured, professional environment. The organization, now the world's largest referral network, has tens of thousands of members on every populated continent of the world. Since its inception, members of BNI® have passed millions of referrals, generating billions of dollars in business for the participants.

The primary purpose of the organization is to pass qualified business referrals to the members. The philosophy of BNI® may be summed up in two simple words: Givers Gain®. If you give business to people, you will get business from them. BNI® allows only one person per profession to join a chapter. The program is designed for businesspeople to develop long-term relationships, thereby creating a basis for trust and, inevitably, referrals. The mission of BNI® is to help members increase their business through a structured, positive, and professional word-of-mouth program that enables them to develop long-term, meaningful relationships with quality business professionals.

To visit a chapter near you, contact BNI® on the Internet at bni@bni.com or visit the Web site at www.bni.com.